Extending

ENGLISH

Series editors:
- Linda Hill
- Zoë Livingstone

Authors:
- Linda Hill
- Zoë Livingstone
- Margaret Ryan
- Saira Sawtell
- Anita Spires
- Pat Woolfe

DL **DYNAMIC LEARNING**
Innovate • Motivate • Personalise
CD-ROM INSIDE

HODDER EDUCATION

The Publishers would like to thank the following for permission to reproduce copyright material:

Photo credits Pg v: © Steve Hill; **Unit 1 image:** used by permission of HarperCollins publishers; **pg 1:** © Photodisc (top photo), © Macmillan Children's Books (bottom photo); **pg 2:** © Photodisc; **pg 3:** © National Gallery Collection. By kind permission of the Trustees of the National Gallery, London/CORBIS; **pg 5:** © Kirsty McLaren/Alamy; **pg 6:** © Visual Arts Library (London)/Alamy; **pg 7:** ALBERTO CRISTOFARI A3/eyevine; **pg 9:** © Macmillan Children's Books; **pg 10:** © Bill Haber/AP/PA Photos; **pg 11:** www.topfoto.co.uk; **pg 13:** used by kind permission of UNICEF; **pg 14:** Lewis Whyld/PA Wire/PA Photos (left photo), © Klaus Hackenberg/zefa/Corbis (right photo); **pg 16:** © Kathy de Witt/Lebrecht Music & Arts/Corbis; **pg 17:** © Robin Whalley/LOOP IMAGES/Loop Images/Corbis (top photo), © Niall McDiarmid/Alamy (bottom photo); **pg 21:** Maggie Hardie/Rex Features (left photo), © Tatu/Alamy (right photo); **pg 22:** Pictorial Press Ltd/Alamy; **pg 23:** © North Wind Picture Archives/Alamy (top photo), © photoalto (middle and bottom photos); **pg 24:** © Lebrecht Music and Arts Photo Library/Alamy; **pg 25:** © Mary Evans Picture Library/Alamy; **pg 26:** Mark Bolton/ Garden Picture Library/photolibrary.com (top photo), © V&A Images/Alamy (bottom photo); **pg 27:** The Bridgeman Art Library/Getty Images (top photo), © Mary Evans Picture Library/Alamy; **pg 28:** Joel Ryan/PA Archive/PA Photos; **pg 29:** Rex Features (top photo), © DAVID NEWHAM/Alamy (bottom photo); **pg 30:** © Visual Arts Library (London)/Alamy (top photo), © North Wind Picture Archives/Alamy (bottom photo); **Unit 4 image:** © 2008 Espresson Education Limited (trading as Channel 4 Learning); **pg 32:** © Tom Grill/Corbis; **pg 34:** © John Springer Collection/CORBIS; **pg 38:** © 2008 Espresson Education Limited (trading as Channel 4 Learning); **pg 40:** Photodisc/Photolibrary.com; **pg 42:** © Mary Evans Picture Library/Alamy; **pg 43:** © Mary Evans Picture Library/Alamy; **pg 44:** FPG/Taxi/Getty Images (top photo), © Alex Segre/Alamy (bottom photo); **pg 45:** Robin Bartholik/UpperCut Images/Getty Images (top photo), used by kind permission of responsibletravel.com (bottom photo); **pg 46:** www.topfoto.co.uk; **pg 47:** Paul Brown/Rex Features (left photo), PA Archive/PA Photos (right photo); **pg 48:** © Fred Prouser/Reuters/CORBIS (top photo), James Devaney/WireImage/Getty Images (bottom photo); **pg 49:** © CORBIS (top photo), Empics Entertainment/Jeff Moore/PA Photos (bottom photo); **pg 50:** Photodisc; **Unit 6 image:** © JLImages/Alamy; **pg 51:** www.purestockX.com; **pg 54:** © Paul A. Souders/CORBIS (top photo), © imagebroker/Alamy (bottom left photo), © Photofusion Picture Library/Alamy (bottom right photo); **pg 55:** Momatiuk - Eastcott/Corbis; **pg 56:** © DreamWorks Distribution LLC/Special Anti-Pesto Still (Aardman/Bureau L.A. Collection/Corbis); **pg 57:** © Mark J. Barrett/Alamy; **pg 58:** © Matthias Kulka/zefa/Corbis (left photo), © Krzysztof Gebarowski – fotolia.com (right photo); **pg 60:** © Eureka/Alamy; **Unit 7 image:** © Lebrecht Music and Arts Photo Library/Alamy; **pg 61:** Roy Rainford/Robert Harding World Imagery/Getty Images; **pg 62:** © Kirsty McLaren/Alamy; **pg 63:** Dave Bradley Photography/Taxi/Getty Images; **pg 64:** © PCL/Alamy; **pg 65:** © Martin Harvey/Alamy; **pg 66:** © Rune Hellestad/Corbis; **pg 67:** UPPA/www.topfoto.co.uk; **pg 72:** © Robert Harding Picture Library Ltd/Alamy; **pg 73:** Joy Skipper/photolibrary.com; **pg 74:** © Paul A. Souders/CORBIS; **pg 75–77:** © TUI UK, by kind permission of Thomson UK Ltd; **Unit 9 image:** © Photodisc; **pg 82:** © Jutta Klee/CORBIS; **pg 83:** © Fred de Noyelle/Godong/Corbis; **pg 84:** © Adam Woolfitt/CORBIS; **pg 86:** Photodisc; **pg 87:** © Allan Ivy/Alamy; **pg 88:** © Wolfgang Kaehler/CORBIS; **pg 89:** © David Pollack/CORBIS; **pg 90:** © William Taufic/CORBIS.

Acknowledgements Unit 1: from *Framed* by Frank Cottrell Boyce (Macmillan Children's Books, 2005), reprinted by permission of the publisher; **pg 1:** from *Millions* by Frank Cottrell Boyce (Macmillan Children's Books, 2004), reprinted by permission of the publisher; **pg 10:** from *Harry Potter and the Deathly Hallows* by J. K. Rowling (Bloomsbury, 2008), reprinted by permission of the author c/o Christopher Little Literary Agency; **pg 14:** from *The Long Walk to Freedom* by Nelson Mandela (Abacus, 1995), reprinted by permission of Little, Brown Book Group; **pg 34:** from *Kensuke's Kingdom* by Michael Morpurgo (Heineman Young Books, 1999), reprinted by permission of Egmont UK Ltd; **pg 46:** from 'The Drum Major Instinct' speech by Martin Luther King, Ebenezer Baptist Church, Atlanta, Georgia, February 4, 1968; **pg 48:** song lyrics from *It's my Life* by Jon Bon Jovi (Island Records); song lyrics by Mark Hollis and Tim Friese-Greene from *It's My Life*, recorded by No Doubt, from *The Singles 1992-2003* album (Interscope, 2003); **pg 49:** from *'We Shall Fight on the Beaches'* speech by Winston Churchill, House of Commons, June 4, 1940; from acceptance speech as Prime Minister by Gordon Brown, 17 May, 2007; **pg 51:** RSPCA pet care: Rabbits, www.rspca.org.uk, courtesy of the RSPCA; **pg 53:** Epson Stylus Photo 790 advertisement, reproduced by kind permission of Epson and Leo Burnett Worldwide Inc.; **pg 56:** transcript from *Wallace & Gromit: The Curse of the Were-Rabbit* trailer (2005), reproduced by permission of Aardman Animations; **pg 57:** 'Having A Ball...' by David Wilkes, *Daily Mail* (24 August, 2007), reproduced by permission of Solo Syndication; **pg 59:** from *Animal Farm* by George Orwell, © George Orwell 1945, reprinted by permission of Bill Hamilton as the Literary Executor of the Estate of the Late Sonia Brownell Orwell and Secker & Warburg Ltd; transcript of voiceover from *Chicken Run* (Aardman, 2000), reproduced by permission DreamWorks Animation; **pg 60:** from *The Hobbit* by J.R.R. Tolkien (1937), reprinted by permission of HarperCollins Publishers; **pg 66:** from *Raven's Gate* by Anthony Horowitz (Walker Books, 2005), text © 2005 Stormbreaker Productions Ltd, reproduced by permission of Walker Books Ltd, London SE11 5HJ; **pg 71:** Machu Ado about deepest Peru webpage from www.travelmail.co.uk, reproduced by permission of Solo Syndication; **pg 72:** Globedecker blog, reproduced by permission of Todd Decker and TravelPod; **pg 73:** Podcast extract by Simon Calder, reproduced by permission of The Independent; **pg 87:** British Citizenship Oath, following the Nationality, Immigration & Asylum Act, 2002, © Crown copyright; **pg 90:** from 'Sydney for Olympic Games of 2000', www.nostos.com, reproduced by permission of Nostos.com.

Although every effort has been made to ensure that website addresses are correct at time of going to press, Hodder Education cannot be held responsible for the content of any website mentioned in this book. It is sometimes possible to find a relocated web page by typing in the address of the home page for a website in the URL window of your browser.

Hachette Livre UK's policy is to use papers that are natural, renewable and recyclable products and made from wood grown in sustainable forests. The logging and manufacturing processes are expected to conform to the environmental regulations of the country of origin.

Orders: please contact Bookpoint Ltd, 130 Milton Park, Abingdon, Oxon OX14 4SB.
Telephone: (44) 01235 827720. Fax: (44) 01235 400454. Lines are open 9.00–5.00, Monday to Saturday, with a 24-hour message answering service. Visit our website at www.hoddereducation.co.uk

© 2008 Hill, Livingstone, Ryan, Sawtell, Spires, Woolfe

First published in 2008 by
Hodder Education,
Part of Hachette Livre UK
338 Euston Road
London NW1 3BH

Impression number   5 4 3 2 1

Year   2013 2012 2011 2010 2009 2008

Cover photo © Pierre Tostee/Covered Images via Getty Images

Illustrations by Andy Roberts and Oxford Illustrators and Designers Ltd

Typeset in Avenir 45 Book, 11/14pt by 2ibooks [publishing solutions] Cambridge

Printed in Italy

A catalogue record for this title is available from the British Library

ISBN: 978 0 340 94886 6

Extending

Contents

Extending

UNIT 5 Speaking and listening: Developing communication skills

UNIT 6 Writing: Saving the animals

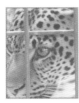

UNIT 7 Shakespeare: *Macbeth*

UNIT 8 Multimodality: Travel texts

UNIT 9 Research and presentation: Multicultural Britain

Extending

Introduction

During this **Interactive English** course your teacher will introduce you to a wide range of activities and resources to help your learning and skills in English. You may use an interactive whiteboard, handouts, webpages, podcasts or film clips from the Dynamic Learning resource bank. Sometimes you will work on your own, and at other times in a pair, in a group or as a part of the whole class.

▲ The Dynamic Learning lesson launch screen (Lesson 5 in Unit 1). You may be using this as part of your class lesson.

▲ Working on the Pupil's Book in pairs. (Lesson 5 in Unit 1).

This **Pupil's Book** is designed to help you work independently to build on the skills you are learning in lessons. You may be asked to use this book in class or on your own at home. You will also find interactive versions of the pages of this book on the Dynamic Learning CD inside the book. There are other resources on the CD too – like audio clips, presentations and links to websites.

Wherever you use this book – at home or in school – think carefully about how it links to what you have learned in the class lesson and be prepared to tell others what you have learned.

Extending

1.1 Team Hughes

Being a reading detective

Sometimes, the writer of a novel does not tell us directly what the characters are like. We need to use clues to figure them out. When we start reading *Framed*, we need to read closely and look at the clues to work out what characters such as Dylan and Dad are like.

Ideas about Dad	The clues!	Ideas about Dylan
Creative, quick thinking, clever Kind – doesn't want to embarrass Dylan Gentle and reassuring	Like the time when we were at Prestatyn and Minnie wanted a swim but I wouldn't get in the water because it was too cold. She kept saying, 'Come in. It's fine once you're in.' And I kept saying, 'No.' Dad got up, went to the caravan and came back with a kettle of boiling water. He poured the water in the sea and said, 'Dylan, come and test it. Tell me if it's all right or does it need a bit more? I said, 'No, that's fine now, thanks, Dad.' 'Sure now?' 'Sure now.'	Little bit of a wimp? Gullible – but trusts his dad

One thing about me is that <u>I always really try to do whatever Dad tells me. So I was excellent first lesson.</u>

Mr Quinn was doing 'People We Admire' for Art. A huge boy with a freckly neck nominated Sir Alex Ferguson and listed all the trophies United had won under his stewardship. Mr Quinn was looking around the room. <u>I put my hand up. He asked a girl.</u>

'Oh. Don't know, sir.'

<u>I used my other hand to hoist my hand up higher.</u>

'Damian, who do you admire?'

By now, most of the others were into players versus managers.

I said, 'St Roch, sir.'

<u>The others stopped talking.</u>

'Who does he play for?'

<u>'No one, sir. He's a saint.'</u>

The others went back to football.

'He caught the plague and hid in the woods so he wouldn't infect anyone, and a dog came and fed him every day. Then he started to do miraculous cures and people came to see him – hundreds of people – in his hut in the woods. He was so worried about saying the wrong thing to someone that he didn't say a word for the last ten years of his life.'

'We could do with a few like him in this class. <u>Thank you, Damian.</u>'

'He's the patron saint of plague, cholera and skin complaints. While alive, he performed many wonders.'

'Well, you learn something new.'

<u>He was looking for someone else now, but I was enjoying being excellent.</u>

In this extract from *Millions*, another novel by Frank Cottrell Boyce, we are introduced to the character Damian.

CHALLENGE >>

1 Draw up a table with three columns. The first column is for you to list the underlined text on the left. The second is to record how impressive Damian imagined he was being in the places underlined. The third is to record what the class probably thought of him.

2 Imagine Mr Quinn, the teacher, keeps a record of all his pupils. What would be his first impressions of Damian based on the above passage? Write notes for a brief report.

1.2 Marvellous Manod

Frank Cottrell Boyce uses a range of techniques to make his writing interesting and engaging for the reader.

For example, this is how he describes the lights of the Nissan on top of the mountain:

> But the cars kept going well past the Sellwoods' place. We could see the smudges of headlights every now and then as they worked their way up the twisty road. Then suddenly a streak of light punched into the clouds, right up near the top. Everyone went, 'Wow!' all together. The light stayed there, sticking and spreading out, **like a frozen firework**.
>
> Minnie said, '**Like some strange alien searchlight** scanning the skies for a long-lost mother ship!'
>
> I said, 'That's the Nissan. It's got safari lights mounted on the roof rack. And a heated glove compartment so you can keep your takeaway warm.'
>
> And Tom said, 'Cowabunga!'

Because the narrator is Dylan, and he sees things slightly differently from other people, his similes, metaphors and descriptions tend to be quite amusing and light, rather than sounding very poetic and serious.

CHALLENGE >>>

1 Have a look at the descriptions from a later chapter below. Dylan's language has been blanked out. See if you can guess which of the choices in the next column show the actual language Dylan used.
2 What is it about your choices that made you think they were Dylan's words?
  > How do they affect the mood and tone of the description?
  > What do they add that the others do not?
  > What do they tell us about him?
3 Imagine Mr Lester was working out similes and metaphors to fit the gaps. What might he come up with?

Dylan's description	Choices
I know it sounds exciting, driving through cloud, but it's actually like driving through lots of _____.	• murky dark fog • dirty grey dishcloths • mysterious dark shadows
We drove at _____ speed through the murky air.	• a very slow • a crawling • lamb
Even the slate didn't look grey any more. It was blue-black and silvery, like _____.	• a beetle's shiny shell • the shimmering water in a well • an old Mercedes with a new wax finish
Out of the back window all you could see was this dirty, thick _____ of cloud stuffed into the valley.	• duvet • layer • cushion
The road ahead was just like a _____ of tarmac …	• narrow track • streak • dribble
… with grass growing down the middle of it, like _____.	• a really long Mohican • a challenge against technology • the rebellious hair on a boar's back

1.3 Mystery up the mountain

Later in the novel, Dylan is shown a painting by Michelangelo, *The Manchester Madonna.* He seems particularly unimpressed and describes it like this:

> It was a picture, a picture of a woman trying to read a book. The woman's face was in colour, but her clothes were in black and white and the top of her head was missing. The most random thing though was that one of her boobies was sticking out of her dress, like you sometimes see on the front of the papers … You could make out the outlines of two other people in the background, waiting to be coloured in like in a colouring book or like they were just materialising on a teleporter platform.

Compare this with the language Mr Lester uses to describe the painting:

> As you can see, the painting is unfinished. The Madonna's clothes are … blocked out in black, but one assumes they were going to be painted blue. Somehow it adds to the drama. As if the master was in such a hurry to capture the perfection of this girl's face, he couldn't wait for the paint to arrive …

▶ The sky in the background …

▶ Her eyes looked down as though …

▶ The boy reached out like …

▶ She stood there like …

▶ Her dress was the pink of …

▶ The characters in the background looked like …

▶ The ground they stood on was the green of …

CHALLENGE >>

1 Pick out the details from both of these texts that you think show the difference in style between Dylan and Mr Lester and say why they are typical of each person's ways of speaking.
2 Take Dylan's extract and rewrite it in the form of a dialogue with Mr Lester. Imagine that after every sentence that Dylan says, your teacher interrupts to comment or clarify. What would they say?

CHALLENGE >>

> Look at the picture of *The Manchester Madonna.* Finish off the statements with a simile, a metaphor, or another piece of description, in a way that you think Dylan might say it.
> Repeat this exercise, but this time try to describe the painting using Mr Lester's style.
> Then try to decide which set of descriptions, Dylan's or Mr Lester's, would bring the painting most to life for a person who had never seen it but was being told about it.

Extending

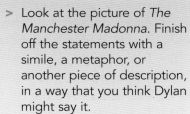

1.4 Don't count your chickens

The family in *Framed* seem to be having a difficult time. Just when things start to get better, something else bad happens!

Lots of writers keep us involved in the story by changing the **tension**. Sometimes, when things are going badly, we become very tense as readers – we are 'on the edge of our seat' wondering what will happen. We want to keep reading to find out! Normally, at the height of the story, it becomes very tense and dramatic, and then all the problems are sorted out.

Think about the summary below of the story of *The Three Little Pigs*:

1   The three little pigs live together with their mum.
2   She decides that they need to leave home, but warns them about the wolf.
3   They meet a man with some straw, and the first pig decides to build a straw house.
4   They meet a man with sticks, and the second pig decides to build a stick house.
5   The third pig decides it would be better to build a brick house.
6   The wolf arrives at the straw house and asks to come in. When refused, he threatens to blow the house down.
7   The wolf blows the house down and eats the pig.
8   The wolf arrives at the stick house and asks to come in. When refused, he threatens to blow the house down.
9   The wolf blows the house down and eats the pig.
10 The wolf tries to do the same at the brick house, but cannot blow it down.
11 The wolf pretends to be friendly to the pig, tells him about where he has seen some nice turnips, and invites him to go with him to get some.
12 The clever pig sneaks out early and gets the turnips on his own.
13 The wolf turns up and finds out he has been tricked – he is furious!
14 He decides to climb down the chimney to eat the pig.
15 The pig has put the turnips on to cook on the fire, and the wolf climbs straight into the boiling pot.
16 The wolf dies, and the pig survives.

CHALLENGE >>>

1   Create a graph, and number the bottom axis from 1 to 16. The vertical axis represents tension in the story.
    Draw a point on the graph for each of the 16 story events according to how tense it is, and then join up the dots.
2   Look at the way the tension rises and falls in this simple children's story. Imagine you have been given the task of making it more interesting and exciting, and giving it a steadier rise in tension. Allow yourself 20 story events to improve it.
3   Now draw a graph to represent your new story and compare it with your original graph. How different is it?

1.5 The power of paintings

The dialogue in *Framed* is very important. Very often, there is much more to what the characters say than what is on the surface. Also, we can often tell what the characters are thinking – this is because of the narrative, as well as what they say.

For example, look at this conversation between Terrible Evans, Minnie and Dylan.

> 'It isn't real is it?' said Terrible. 'Is it a photograph or what?'
>
> 'It's a painting,' said Minnie, and then she said very quietly to me, 'and it's not by Michelangelo.'
>
> I whispered, 'Thanks.'

If this were a script for a play, it might be written like this:

(The children all gather around the painting. Minnie stares in horror.)

TERRIBLE: *(Shocked and confused)* It isn't real is it? … Is it a photograph or what?

MINNIE: *(Rolls her eyes and shakes her head)* It's a painting. *(Whispering to Dylan)* … and it's not by Michelangelo.

DYLAN: *(Whispering)* Thanks.

When you are writing a script, you need to remember the following conventions:
- Put the initial stage directions above the script in italics and in brackets.
- Put the character's name in capitals, followed by a colon.
- Before the speech, put any stage directions in brackets and italics. The stage directions could be about the actions, or the tone of voice that should be used.
- Do not use speech marks.
- Write everything in the present tense.

CHALLENGE >>
> Write a short extra scene you might add to a drama adaptation of the novel. Set it on the bus when Ms Stannard sits next to Dylan.
> Dylan questions her on why she says, 'I believe you're a lot cleverer than you let on.' Take it up from that point, bringing out what she knows.

1.6 Paintings are like mutagen

Many of the characters in the novel are transformed by the beauty of the paintings. Can you remember which characters made these comments?

1 It was the oranges that really got me!

2 I used to hate the rain. Imagine how terrible it would be if the rain stopped now.

3 I feel like a million dollars now!

4 There's powerful stuff in those pictures.

This is the painting that had a very powerful effect on Mr Davis:

▲ *Bathers at Grenouillère* by Monet

CHALLENGE >>

Spend some time thinking about the painting.

> Who is in it?
> What are their feelings?
> What sounds, smells and physical sensations would you experience there?
> How would you describe the colours and the light?
> What sorts of things would be going on?

Collect your ideas in a spider diagram. Then turn your notes into a brief paragraph describing this scene.

CHALLENGE >>

Look at the painting and imagine you are describing to a blind person what it looks like and the emotional impact it has on a person viewing it. Write down the most vivid description of it you can, making use of the senses, choosing your words and phrases carefully and including powerful imagery.

1.7 Looking from the wrong angle

Sometimes when we read a text it is clear to see what the writer's viewpoint is. We can see how he or she feels about the characters and the events in the story.

Read the extract below from the 30 June. During this extract, Dylan is attempting to commit a serious crime, and he is betraying someone who has become a friend.

Think about how Frank Cottrell Boyce feels about Dylan's actions.

▲ Frank Cottrell Boyce

Tom was outside school next morning. When he saw me coming, he ran over and shook my hand, and carried on shaking it until I thought my teeth were going to drop out. He kept saying, 'I'm so happy. I'm so happy.'

'Good,' I said. 'Why?'

'Minnie says you have a great plan. She says you're going to put everything back the way it was. I get my job back even!'

'When did she say that?'

Just now. Thank you. Thank you. Thank you.'

'Well, the thing is, she shouldn't have said that …'

'Why? Did you want it to be a surprise?'

'No, but …'

'Dylan. Everywhere I go in this town I see things that you have done. The nice shop windows. The boating lake. The pavilion. The sign. You did all of this to the town. You made the town better. And now you are going to make me better.'

'Well, the thing is …'

'Dylan, you are just like your father. You fix everything.'

…

I'd hardly got to the fence when Lester came out to meet me.

…

He was so pleased to see me, and I'd only come to rob a painting from him. I felt like telling him the truth there and then, but then he said, 'I hear you're moving on?'

'Yeah.'

'Where to?'

I looked at the exceptional view – at the shiny black peak of Blenau Mountain, at the green slopes of Manod Mountain, at the big duvet of cloud that covered my town. Were we really going to go away and leave it all? I took a deep breath and said, 'Did you ever hear of a painting called *Sunflowers*?'

CHALLENGE >>

1 There are three speakers in this extract: Tom and Mr Lester, who are clearly happy about events, and Dylan, the narrator, who is not. Write down words and phrases that give us insight into each character's mood.
2 Dylan does not actually say very much in this extract. Think about what he must be really thinking, yet unable to say, and then:
   > Suggest reasons why he does not share the other two people's optimism.
   > Discuss what he must be thinking, knowing they are going to be disappointed with him.

CHALLENGE >>

In this book the author, Frank Cottrell Boyce, repeatedly makes a point that art is something that can transform and improve a person's life. From what you have learned so far, write a letter supporting the author's viewpoint to a friend who you know thinks art is a waste of time.

1.8 The perfect crime?

When you are working in a group, it is important that everyone makes suggestions and comments, asks questions, and tries to bring all the ideas from the group together.

In Year 7:

- Pupils who are **just starting to develop their speaking and listening** skills will sometimes add to what other people say, but their comments are not always totally relevant to the topic or task. They will sometimes ask questions and offer new ideas.
- Quite **competent speakers and listeners** will make quite a few relevant points, and will build on what other people say. They will take on different roles in the group without any help.
- Very **confident speakers and listeners** will take a leading role in the group, moving the discussion in a clear direction, encouraging others to talk and sorting out disagreements.

Below is a transcript from a group who are trying to create a tower out of paper and sticky tape.

Parminder:	So … um … any ideas about what the best way will be to build this tower?
Hayley:	They had a big tower in that film … what's it called … *Men in Black*. The big insect climbed up and no one could catch it.
Jude:	Yeh! I remember that one. Will Smith had to climb up and everything.
Parminder:	Mmmm … but what about *our* tower? We've got how many … six sheets of paper … and this tape.
Jude:	Why don't we try rolling them into a big long tube?
Parminder:	That might work … Good idea.
Jude:	We could sellotape the bottom of it to the desk to hold it up.
Hayley:	That's a rubbish idea. It will fall over.
Parminder:	But it would be tall. How could we make it stronger down here?
Jude:	Maybe we could use one sheet to make some supports there …

CHALLENGE >>

- > Who do you think is the strongest speaker in the group?
- > Which group members listen most carefully?
- > Which person helps to move the discussion along, and how?
- > Write out a list of the ways in which the weakest speaker could improve.

CHALLENGE >>

Use the same speakers and introduce one more person who is deliberately being unhelpful. Write a new dialogue beginning with the new person saying, 'This whole thing is stupid'. The other speakers should explain why the task of building a tower is worthwhile.

1.9 Zebras are not impossible

Below is a review written about Frank Cottrell Boyce's other novel, *Millions*:

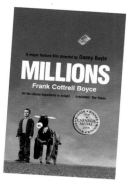

Frank Cottrell Boyce has already proved his worth as a screenwriter, but his first children's novel *Millions* is a definite success. ❶ This delightful and thought provoking story works on a number of levels. It has charmed readers of all ages and there are already plans to make it into a film.

The story follows two young boys who accidentally stumble across a quarter of a million pounds of stolen money, and have only seventeen days in which to try and spend it. ❷

Undoubtedly, the key to its success is the endearing narrator Damian. He is a sweet and thoughtful boy, determined to do good, who rarely understands the full meaning of what he is saying, ❸ and this is often where much of the humour comes from. For example, at school, Damian tells the class ❹ all the gory details of the various saints he is obsessed with. He takes his teacher's repetition of, 'Thank you, Damian,' (meaning 'Be quiet Damian') ❺ as great encouragement and keeps going. As he says, 'I was enjoying being excellent.' We know that he a little bit different to the others, but he doesn't, and that makes us love him all the more.

The other real strength of the novel is not just the humour of Damian's narrative, but the serious emotional journey that we go through with him as the novel progresses. ❻ Damian's obsession with the saints is amusing, but we quickly realise that there is a serious side to it, and that Damian and his family are gradually coming to terms with the very sad loss of his mother. ❼ The beauty of the novel is that way that Boyce handles this sensitively and balances it with fun and adventure.

In addition to this the novel makes us think about broader issues, such as the value and importance of money. Older brother Anthony can't wait to spend it on luxuries and riches, but Damian has a more noble cause in mind. He thinks that the money has been sent by God, 'I suppose you could call it a sign, A big loud sign.' The trouble that this money causes makes the reader think hard about the value of cash.

This novel has everything: excitement, humour, and a strong and loveable narrator. ❽ But most of all it is the fact that it is such a touching family story that makes it a compelling read.

CHALLENGE >>

1 For each of the paragraphs in this review, identify the topic sentence which tells us what the whole paragraph is all about.
2 This review contains a range of features that you can use in your own writing. Can you match the numbered features to the explanations at the bottom of the page?
3 Write the topic sentences for a review of *Framed*.

A	The review talks about the writer's techniques and style.
B	The review avoids giving too much away about the plot.
C	Main points are backed up with examples or further explanation.
D	The present tense is used to talk about events in the novel.
E	An introduction which might comment on the overall quality of the novel or the writer.
F	Direct quotes from the novel are used to back up ideas – with speech marks.
G	Powerful adjectives are used when describing aspects of the novel.
H	Linking phrases or connectives are used to link from one paragraph to another.

Extending

1.10 Writing a review

Here is another review, this time of the last of the Harry Potter novels, *Harry Potter and the Deathly Hallows*.

CHALLENGE >>

Read through this review with a partner, identify its topic sentences and see if you can pick out any of the features from the checklist on the previous page.

The Final Chapter: Harry Potter and the Deathly Hallows by J. K. Rowling

Thousands of fans dressed up: donned their stripy tights and pointy hats, and headed for supermarkets and bookshops kept open until midnight across the country. At last the final instalment they had been waiting for was here. But will they be disappointed? Is this the best Harry Potter novel so far?

It is certainly the most exciting, fast paced and action packed. Rowling has not disappointed when it comes to drama. The epic battles that take place between the forces of good and evil continue to amaze and thrill readers. At one point in the novel, Voldemort's evil hordes invade the school, resulting in a scene of cataclysmic destruction. Rowling's description of the scene chills the blood. '… the world resolved itself into pain and semi–darkness: he was half-buried in the wreckage of a corridor that had been subjected to a terrible attack; cold air told him that the side of the castle had been blown away and hot stickiness on his cheek told him that he was bleeding copiously.'

It is not only the action packed pace that keeps the reader on the edge of their seat, but also the darkness that pervades every page. This sets it apart from those that went before. Gone are the teen romances and chocolate frogs of previous novels: the dark shadow of Voldemort has rid the world of such innocent fancies. Some might argue that this makes the novel unsuitable for Rowling's young readers, but in fact it is what makes it so perfect. The original fans have not outgrown the novels, the novels have grown up with them.

In addition to this, the way Rowling has managed to resolve all of the sub-plots and mysteries will also satisfy her most avid fans. She has always claimed that the whole series has been carefully mapped out and planned, and this novel seems to provide the proof. Even the mystery of Severus Snape and where his true loyalties lie is finally laid to rest. This is particularly important for Potter fans who pride themselves on knowing every little detail about the characters, and Rowling does not let them down.

The only disappointment likely to strike the pointy hatted masses is that they will have to face the reality that this really is the last one.

CHALLENGE > >

Be a critic.

> Either:
  Write a review of *Framed*, saying what it is about and detailing its strengths and why it appeals to readers your age.
> Or:
  Write or plan a review of a novel or film which you have not liked. Explain why you are not impressed with it and bring out its weaknesses. Make it clear that your objections are fair and justified.

For suggestions and reviews of newly-published novels try some of these websites:

www.carnegiegreenaway.org.uk/shadowingsite

www.booktrusted.co.uk/books

www.channel4learning.net/sites/bookbox

2.1 The real me

Many people, not always particularly famous, have chosen to write about themselves. The most common format for these people is the autobiography, but many people have chosen to publish letters they have written, or their diaries.

Historians often find these particularly useful, because they tell them about the events of the past. Two of the most famous diarists are Samuel Pepys and Anne Frank.

Samuel Pepys

Samuel Pepys lived and worked in London in the years following Oliver Cromwell's death in 1658. They were turbulent times and there was a great deal for Pepys to write about. This was probably one of the reasons he began his diary.

Because of his connections with people in important positions, his diary has provided historians with a great deal of information about the times, including the Great Fire of London. Read the extract on the right where Pepys describes the fire.

Anne Frank

Anne was a young Jewish girl who lived in Amsterdam at the start of World War II. In May 1942, a few weeks before her 13th birthday, she was given a diary as a birthday present.

Her diary mainly deals with her time in the 'secret annexe'. This was the name people have given to the place where Anne had to go into hiding with her parents, her sister and four other Jewish people. It was wartime, and The Netherlands was occupied by the German army. Jewish people were being arrested and sent to concentration camps.

By and by Jane comes and tells me that she hears that above 300 houses have been burned down tonight by the fire we saw … So I … walked to the Tower; and there got up upon one of the high places, … and there I did see the houses at the end of the bridge all on fire, and an infinite great fire on this and the other side … of the bridge … it began this morning in the King's baker's house in Pudding Lane, and that it hath burned St. Magnus's Church and most part of Fish Street already. So I rode down to the waterside, … and there saw a lamentable★ fire … Everybody endeavouring to remove their goods, and flinging into the river … poor people staying in their houses as long as till the very fire touched them, and then running into boats, or clambering from one pair of stairs by the waterside to another.

★lamentable = very bad and depressing

CHALLENGE > >

Use the internet and other resources to find out more about Anne Frank. Use the information you find to write a 150-word article for a children's encyclopaedia on Anne Frank and her diary.

CHALLENGE > >

Imagine that for some reason you and your family are going to have to go into hiding. Write two brief diary entries, one written immediately before going into hiding and the other recording your feelings one month later.

Extending

2.2 Information texts

We are all bombarded with information all day, every day: from people, from television, radio, newspapers, and dozens of other sources. Not all information comes in the form of words, however. What are these symbols and images telling you?

CHALLENGE >>>

Now devise signs to represent the following information:
> Please turn off your mobile phone before the show starts.
> Do not walk on the grass.
> This restaurant only serves vegetarian food.
> Watch out, there's a thief about.
> Protect the planet.

Sometimes we need to find information for ourselves. Fortunately, there are usually plenty of places where you can find what you need. Where would you look or go to find out the information listed in the left-hand column below?

Match each item with a source of information in the right-hand column.

- where to buy special balloons for a party
- some places of interest to take a visitor to your area
- recipe for chocolate cake
- times of trains to and from a neighbouring town
- what's on television tonight
- who said … ?
- meaning of a word
- what's on at your local cinema

- dictionary of quotations
- train timetable
- TV guide
- dictionary
- local newspaper
- Yellow Pages
- Tourist Information Centre
- cookery book

Of course, much of this information can now be found on the internet – the information superhighway. Before the internet, many people relied on encyclopedias to provide them with information.

★ Encyclopaedia Britannica

★ The *Encyclopaedia Britannica* was first published in 1768 and is the oldest and most respected encyclopedia in English that is still published. It is aimed at educated adult readers and is written by a staff of 19 full-time editors and more than 4,000 expert contributors.

CHALLENGE > >

Sales of encyclopedias have greatly reduced in recent years, probably because of the easy availability of sources of information online. Imagine that you are the editor of an encyclopedia, trying to come up with ideas to boost sales. Try to find five reasons to persuade young people to ask their parents to buy them an encyclopedia.

2.3 Planning an interview

In Lesson 3 with the class, you will be thinking about planning an interview in order to find out about older people's childhoods. It might help you to think about the rights of children and to consider whether these have changed since your interviewee's childhood.

UNICEF unicef

In your class Lesson 2, we looked at the UNICEF report on how happy children are in different countries. But what is UNICEF?

The United Nations Children's Fund was created in December 1946 by the United Nations. It aimed to provide food, clothing and health care to children facing famine and disease after World War II.

UNICEF believes that every child should have clean water, food, health care, education, and a safe environment in which to grow up. The UN Convention on the Rights of the Child (1989) is the framework for all of UNICEF's work on behalf of children. The convention sets out the specific rights of children and their need for special care and assistance. It requires that nations act in the best interests of the child. No other human rights convention has ever attained such widespread agreement, nor so quickly.

UNICEF believes children have a right to:
- protection from violence, abuse, hazardous employment, exploitation, abduction or sale
- special protection in times of war, and no child under 15 should ever have to fight in an army
- protection from disease and famine
- free compulsory primary education
- adequate health care
- equal treatment regardless of gender, race or cultural background
- freedom to express opinions and be listened to
- play.

CHALLENGE >>>

When the Convention on the Rights of the Child was adopted, a number of picture books were published to illustrate each Right. Write the introductory paragraphs of a story to illustrate one of the children's rights listed above that you feel strongly about. Make the story realistic and include dialogue in it.

★ UNICEF Ambassadors

UNICEF appoints Ambassadors, who play a vital role in promoting UNICEF and fundraising on behalf of children. UNICEF's high-profile supporters are in a position to make the world pay attention to the needs of children.

They dedicate time and energy to UNICEF in a variety of ways:
- ★ visiting countries struck by disasters and seeing UNICEF's emergency work in the field
- ★ visiting UNICEF programmes in non-emergency countries.
- ★ speaking to the media about what they have seen
- ★ lobbying and raising money.

Some UNICEF Ambassadors include: Robbie Williams, David Beckham and Shakira.

CHALLENGE >>

Discuss this question either as a whole class or with a partner: What steps would you like to see taken to make the world a better place for children?

Extending

2.4 Writing a good paragraph

In your class Lesson 4, you will be practising writing good paragraphs, based on your likes and dislikes. You should start to think about how games and toys have changed over the years.

Children at play

The Toy of the Year Awards are presented to coincide with the British Toy Fair in January each year. On the right are some of the winners over the past four decades. How many do you remember? What do you think this year's winner will be?

Children's games do change in popularity. However, there is an amazing similarity in some of the games that have been played by children all over the world, and over many years.

Nelson Mandela

This is an extract from Nelson Mandela's autobiography, *The Long Walk to Freedom*.

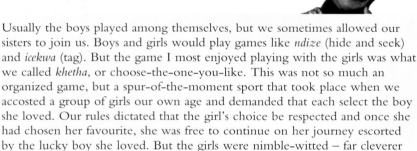

Usually the boys played among themselves, but we sometimes allowed our sisters to join us. Boys and girls would play games like *ndize* (hide and seek) and *icekwa* (tag). But the game I most enjoyed playing with the girls was what we called *khetha*, or choose-the-one-you-like. This was not so much an organized game, but a spur-of-the-moment sport that took place when we accosted a group of girls our own age and demanded that each select the boy she loved. Our rules dictated that the girl's choice be respected and once she had chosen her favourite, she was free to continue on her journey escorted by the lucky boy she loved. But the girls were nimble-witted – far cleverer than we doltish lads – and would often confer among themselves and choose one boy, usually the plainest fellow, and then tease him all the way home.

Many people think that children have fewer opportunities to play these days, because of fears about health and safety. Below is one person's letter to a newspaper on the subject.

The sad part of the health and safety culture is the impact that it has on children. As a child, on the weekends and during the holidays, we had complete freedom to do as we pleased … We lived near some woods that included a military assault course. At the age of 5 or so, we were climbing on the course, sliding down the pulleys, often at really great heights. We knew that if we fell we would be hurt – but that was part of the fun … we had a sense of the danger and risk, and it was worth it.

Toy of the Year Awards

- 1965: James Bond Aston Martin die-cast car
- 1966: Action Man
- 1968: Sindy
- 1973: Mastermind – board game
- 1974: Lego Family set
- 1980: Rubik's Cube
- 1982: Star Wars
- 1985: Transformers (Optimus Prime)
- 1990: Teenage Mutant Ninja Turtles
- 1991: Nintendo GameBoy
- 1994: Power Rangers
- 1996: Barbie
- 1997: Teletubbies
- 1998: Furby
- 2002: Beyblades
- 2004: Robosapien
- 2005: Tamagotchi Connexion

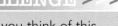

▲ Rubik's Cube

CHALLENGE > >

What do you think of this letter? Write a balanced reply, taking into consideration a wide range of issues. Include in your reply the fact that children these days have got other, more sophisticated ways of entertaining themselves.

2.5 Sharing the findings

In your class Lesson 5, you will be sharing the findings of your interviews. You might be surprised by some of the jobs and things the interviewees were expected to do.

Children at work

These days there are strict rules about the age at which young people can work. Look at the panel on the right.

> **CHALLENGE >>>**
>
> Why do you think the laws are so strict? Do you agree with them?

Things were very different in the past

At the age at which children these days start secondary school, poor children in late 18th-century Lancashire started working 12 to 15 hours a day in the cotton mills. The wages were low, especially for the apprentices, who worked for little more than their board and lodgings. On the right is an extract from *The Factory Lad, or the Life of Simon Smike* – a first-hand account of the experiences of children in the factory system.

> **CHALLENGE >>>**
>
> 1 Use the internet or an encyclopaedia to research more information about the type of work that children did in the 19th century.
> 2 Now write a diary account of one poor child you imagine working in very hard conditions.

> **CHALLENGE >>>**
>
> Imagine you were a workhouse child in the 19th century forced to work long hours in a factory. Write a letter to someone in authority, for example the factory owner or the Prime Minister, outlining why it is wrong to make children work in these conditions. Make out a case to abolish the practice of including children in the labour force.

Specific hours of work allowed
13 and 14 years

Term time

Maximum 12 hours in any 7-day week. Maximum 2 hours on ANY school day (1 hour after 7a.m. and before beginning of school day plus 1 hour after the end of the school day and before 7p.m.) OR 2 hours after the end of the school day and before 7p.m. Saturday maximum 5 hours (1-hour break after 4 hours' continuous work). Sunday maximum 2 hours.

Holidays

Maximum 25 hours per 7-day week (5 hours in any one day) (Sunday 2 hours only)

Simon was quite right when he said the slaves on the other side of the seas were better off than the factory slaves. Even when England rang with appeals for their emancipation, … the Manchester manufacturers were petitioning parliament, in 1836, to let children between eleven and thirteen years of age, work sixty-nine hours a week instead of forty-eight – and … in the same year, … an act of our Parliament had been passed by which it was enacted that no black slave should be worked more than forty-five hours in the week, or seven and a half hours a day. It will thus be seen that a full grown slave – a man in the prime of life, could not by law be worked so long as a little female in England of only eleven years old!

Extending

2.6 Writing the report

Children and books

Although many children count watching television as one of their main pastimes, reading is also very popular.

Children can choose from thousands of authors, who write on any number of subjects, but the favourites are still the good storytellers. Among the favourites are:

Jacqueline Wilson

Jacqueline Wilson was born in Bath in 1945. She always wanted to be a writer and wrote her first 'novel' when she was 9. She has been writing full-time all her adult life.

She has won many awards and, in the poll conducted by the BBC, The Big Read, four books by Jacqueline Wilson were in the Top 100: *Double Act, Girls in Love, Vicky Angel* and *The Story of Tracy Beaker*.

J. K. Rowling

J. K. Rowling was born in 1965. She started writing the Harry Potter series during a train journey from Manchester to London King's Cross and, during the next five years, outlined the plots for each book and began writing the first novel. Her aim was to write seven books in the Harry Potter series. The final book in the series, *Harry Potter and the Deathly Hallows*, was published in 2007.

Roald Dahl

Roald Dahl was born in South Wales on 13 September 1916. In World War II, he fought as a fighter pilot, and was badly injured when his plane crashed. His very first children's book, written in 1943, was called *The Gremlins*.

From 1945 until his death, he lived at Gipsy House in Buckinghamshire, where he wrote his famous children's books. He had lots of hobbies – apart from writing! He loved sport, food and wine, and gardening, and he specialised in growing enormous onions. He died in hospital in Oxford, on 23 November 1990.

▲ Jacqueline Wilson

CHALLENGE > >

1 Make a list of your top five children's authors and say briefly why each appeals to you.
2 Name your five all-time favourite novels and briefly explain your choices.
3 Many of the books written by the authors on this page have been adapted for television, or made into films. Write a paragraph explaining why you would either prefer to read the original, or watch the TV or film version.
4 Many people think that children spend too much time watching television, and that it is bad for them. Do you agree? In what ways might watching television be good for children?

2.7 Time capsule

Time capsule

The term 'time capsule' was coined in 1938 at the New York World's Fair, when a capsule designed to keep for 5,000 years was buried. It contained 1,000 photos, a can opener, a man's hat, safety pins and some sheet music. At the Millennium in 2000, many people planned to leave a record of their lives in time capsules.

But preserving things for posterity is not always easy. A car buried in Oklahoma in 1957 as a time capsule to mark the US state's 50th anniversary was unearthed in 2007. Items pulled from the car's boot included a petrol can and some cans of beer. But what was supposed to be a typical woman's handbag, containing lipstick and tranquillisers, was said to resemble a lump of rotten leather.

As a piece of advice, Professor Brian Durrans from the Museum of Mankind, and co-founder of the International Time Capsule Society, says: 'Consider the kind of information that would not otherwise be preserved and that maybe historians of the future will be grateful to you for.' But, perhaps most of all, remember where you put it! Ten thousand capsules have been buried over the last century, but most have been mislaid. The International Time Capsule Society has a list of the most-wanted missing capsules, including one lost under Blackpool Tower.

◀ Hidden treasure: Blackpool Tower hides a lost capsule.

CHALLENGE >>

1 If you were designing the contents of a time capsule to be opened in 5,000 years time, what would be your five major considerations, bearing in mind the need for the items to survive and that so much will be different by then?
2 Write a letter to the producers of *Blue Peter* explaining why you are not very impressed with their efforts so far to leave a message for the future. What do you think they should have included?

★ *Blue Peter*'s time capsules

★ The first *Blue Peter* time capsule was buried on 7 June 1971 by presenters Val Singleton, John Noakes and Peter Purves. It contained a copy of the 1970 *Blue Peter* annual, a set of decimal coins – which were introduced in 1971 – and photographs of the three presenters. The capsule had to be moved in 1984 to another site in the *Blue Peter* garden.

★ A second box was buried alongside it by presenters Simon Groom, Peter Duncan and Janet Ellis in 1984. This box contained hairs from Goldie the labrador, a record of the programme's theme tune and video footage of the moving of dog Petra's statue.

★ In 1971, the presenters asked *Blue Peter* viewers to write in to remind the programme when the time came to unearth the capsule. Nearly 30 years later, the *Blue Peter* office received thousands of reminders from around the world.

★ There is still one *Blue Peter* time capsule remaining – the *Blue Peter* Millennium Time Capsule. As well as containing a *Blue Peter* badge and a history of the programme, it also contains a set of Teletubby dolls, an insulin pen and a France '98 football. The capsule will be opened in 2050.

2.8 My time capsule

These are everyday items from the past. Do you know what they were used for?

The one on the left is a washboard. These were still in use well into the 20th century, but have now been replaced by the washing machine. The second item is an abacus. You may have had a modern version of this when you were very young, to help you learn to count. They originated from ancient Rome, and were used in the same ways that you might use a calculator today.

Many of the items we take for granted today have been invented only in the last 50 years or so. Can you match the inventions below to the right dates? Use the internet to research.

■ non-stick saucepan	1955
■ Automated Teller Machine (cash machine)	1955
■ mobile phone	1955
■ video games	1961
■ MP3 player	1962
■ industrial robot	1962
■ laptop computer	1969
■ communications satellite	1973
■ TV remote control	1981
■ CDs	1986
■ the first digital film	1995
■ microwave oven	1998

Archaeology

Archaeologists are people who find out about the past through their excavations. They build up a picture of life by examining the artefacts (things) they find.

CHALLENGE >>

What is your opinion about the practice of digging things up to try to discover more of the past? Among other things, bear in mind:
> that bodies are often unearthed
> that digging things up can often damage them
> that later generations of archaeologists might well have better methods of discovering and preserving historical items.

CHALLENGE >>

Find out about 'treasure trove' and what exactly you can and cannot keep of what you find. Then write a letter to a newspaper arguing the case for 'finders keepers' (that anything you find should belong to you).

Answer: saucepan – 1955, cash machine – 1969, mobile – 1973, video games – 1962, MP3 player – 1998, robot – 1961, laptop – 1986, satellite – 1955, remote – 1962, CDs – 1981, digital film – 1995, microwave – 1955

2.9 How it works

A picture paints a thousand words

Have you ever helped someone to assemble flat-pack furniture? This often comes with diagrams, but no words. Why do you think this is?

Diagrams can be very helpful when explaining to someone how to do something, but a combination of diagrams and words is often the best way to explain.

Origami: A dove

Origami is the Japanese art of paper folding. The diagrams below show you how to make a dove.

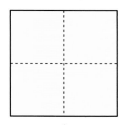

1

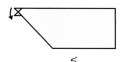

5

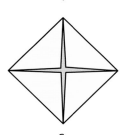

2

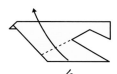

6

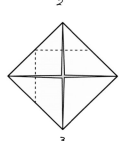

3

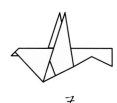

7

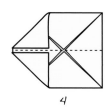

4

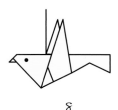

8

CHALLENGE >> >

Add words to make the diagrams below easier to follow.

Some notes to help you:
---------- = fold
————— = edge
———➤ = direction of fold

Note that on **picture 6**, you will need to explain that a piece needs to be cut out to create the tail and wing. On **picture 8**, you will need to explain that the person making the dove, needs to draw two eyes for the dove, and also hang a thread through its back.

CHALLENGE >> >

1 Find some other diagrams and/or instructions for paper toys or items and try to make them.
2 Suggest ways that you think the instructions for making them could be improved.
3 Discuss with a partner what you have learned from the exercises about following instructions.

E x t e n d i n g

2.10 You be the judge

At the beginning of this unit of work, you started by telling your teacher about yourself. Then you chose items to include in your time capsule. Now you might like to include a factfile about your favourite things: books, games, subjects, films, programmes, hobbies, sports, etc.

CHALLENGE >>>

A Day in the Life of...
Imagine you are going to produce a short video to include in your Time Capsule, to explain what the daily life of a child is like today. Describe (or storyboard) six key images that you could include in your video that would help someone to understand what life is like, then add an appropriate commentary. Use a frame like the one below – copy it into your books.

Scene/Image	Description	Commentary

CHALLENGE >>>

Write out a list of instructions that would enable a future generation to operate one of the six items shown in your video. Choose the one that would probably be hardest for someone in the future to use. Use diagrams in addition to your instructions if you think they are necessary.

3.1 'Pay-back Time'

Ballads

Ballads are poems that tell stories. Historically, ballads told stories of great heroes, celebrities of the day and also fairy stories. Ballads have stanzas (verses) with four lines and a simple, repeating rhyming scheme. There is sometimes a refrain at the end of each verse.

Oral tradition

Long before it was common for people to be able to read, they wanted to be able to pass on stories. This was done by singing the stories, and they became ballads.

The rhyming lines were easy to remember, as one person sang it to the next. Because they were rarely written down, each time the story was sung it was likely to change slightly. This is called the oral tradition ('oral' because it was passed on by mouth).

★ Roger McGough

* ★ Roger McGough is a contemporary poet who has written a modern ballad called 'Pay-back Time'.
* ★ Roger McGough has chosen to tell one side of a story that is familiar to all of us – the parent/carer relationship with young people. Certain things are expected of parents and carers, and the poet is having fun telling us how he is not going to be the kind old grandad smoking a pipe quietly in a corner, when he is old.

▲ Kindly parents or carers?

CHALLENGE >>>

1 As you read 'Pay-back Time', try to describe McGough's attitude towards his children. Make a list of everything he tells you about them.
2 Try to write a humorous ballad (or story) entitled 'Now it's my turn to pay you back', in which you remember the times your parents punished you and consider how you will get them back for that.

3.2 'Turpin's Rant'

Highwaymen

The heyday of the 'highwayman' is seen as being the years 1650–1800. A highwayman was a thief on horseback, who usually worked alone and targeted travellers.

The bad state of most of the roads at the time meant that coaches – which were pulled by horses – were restricted to a crawl, especially when travelling uphill. This made them tempting targets for highwaymen. Woodland often provided a hiding place for the highwayman, while the open countryside meant that he could make a speedy escape.

This kind of robbery was most common around London and its approach roads were well known as the haunts of highwaymen. Though most were vicious criminals, the highwayman has passed into folklore as a 'Robin Hood'-type outlaw, to be tolerated if not admired.

★ Heroes or thieves?

* **Robin Hood** is one of the most famous figures from English folktale history. He is an outlaw from medieval times, who is famous for robbing the rich to provide for the poor. He was accompanied by his fellow outlaws – the 'Merry Men' – and they are usually associated with Sherwood Forest and Nottinghamshire. He has been the subject of many books and films.
* **Dick Turpin** (1705–1739) is the most famous highwayman. Although violent, he has been romanticised in English ballads, plays and books, and is often portrayed as a dashing and heroic character. He was executed in York, after being found guilty of murder.

CHALLENGE > >

Can you summarise what it is that has made men such as Robin Hood and Dick Turpin famous? Write down a list of what the two men had in common.

CHALLENGE > >

Robin Hood has been romanticised in stories and films. Imagine they were going to erect a statue in his memory in your town. Write a letter to your local paper objecting to celebrating an outlaw as a hero, and pointing out what kind of man he probably was in reality. You could write instead in the form of a ballad, if you wish.

3.3 'During Wind and Rain'

★ Thomas Hardy

★ The novelist and poet Thomas Hardy (1840–1928) spent most of his life in Dorset. He left school at the age of 16 to become an apprentice to a Dorchester architect. Although he moved to London in 1862 to work for Arthur Blomfield, architect and church restorer, he returned to Dorset in 1867. His first success as a novelist came when he published *Under the Greenwood Tree* in 1872, and the following year he became a full-time novelist.

★ Hardy published a huge number of novels and poems, including the famous novels *Far From the Madding Crowd*, *The Mayor of Casterbridge*, *Tess of the d'Urbervilles* and *Jude the Obscure*. The stories they tell were usually set in the south-west of England in a fictional area Hardy called Wessex.

Mood in poetry

Poets use precise words to create a mood, usually using images. For example, if a poet called the clouds in the sky 'black thunderous weights', we would understand that the mood was gloomy and threatening. By contrast, if a poet called the clouds in the sky 'fluffy cotton-wool balls', we would understand that the mood was joyful and light-hearted.

CHALLENGE >>

What kinds of moods could these types of weather bring about?

HEAVY DOWNPOUR, A FLURRY OF SNOW, FOG, HEATWAVE, LIGHT SHOWER, HEAVY, PERSISTENT SNOW, A WARM BREEZE

CHALLENGE >>

Imagine the mood before some exciting event – for example a party or a football match – and the mood after if it has not been a success. Write down a list of words and phrases that could be used to capture each mood. Then select from your list as you write two paragraphs, capturing the moods before and after the event.

Extending

3.4 'Anthem for Doomed Youth'

★ Wilfred Owen

★ Wilfred Owen (1893–1918) was teaching in France at the beginning of World War I and returned to England in 1915 to enlist in the Artists' Rifles. He received his commission to the Manchester Regiment (5th Battalion) in June 1916, and spent the rest of the year training in England.

★ In January 1917, he was posted to France but in May he was caught in a shell explosion and was diagnosed as having shell-shock. He spent time convalescing near Edinburgh, during which time he wrote a lot of the war poems that have since become so famous.

★ In August 1918, he returned to France. He was awarded the Military Cross for bravery at Amiens, but was killed on 4 November while attempting to lead his men across the Sambre-Oise Canal at Ors. The news of his death reached his parents on 11 November 1918, the day of the Armistice (the end of the war).

World War I

World War I lasted from 1914 to 1918, and is often called The Great War. By 1914, Europe had divided into two camps: the Triple Alliance included Germany, Italy and Austria-Hungary; the Triple Entente included Britain, France and Russia. More than nine million people died during this war and it had a huge, and devastating, impact on the history of the 20th century.

CHALLENGE >>

Talk to your partner about wars which are happening now or which have happened in your lifetime. How many can you come up with? Try to note down where and when the war happened, and who was fighting against whom and when the war happened. Also note down why the war occurred.

CHALLENGE >>

A **pacifist** is someone who refuses to fight in any war because it is morally wrong. Write a conversation between two people about the rights and wrongs of war. One of them believes that in certain circumstances war is justified, whilst the other believes that war can never be justified.

3.5 'If thou must love me'

★ Elizabeth Barrett Browning

★ Elizabeth Barrett Browning (1806–1861) is one of the most respected poets of the Victorian period. In 1845, she met her future husband, the poet Robert Browning, but her father was very difficult and disapproved of their relationship. They had to meet in secret, but eventually they married and then moved to Italy. Elizabeth lived here for most of her life, until her death in 1861.

★ 'If thou must love me' is from a collection of poems written in 1850 called *Sonnets from the Portuguese*, which tells of her own love story with her husband, Robert. In 1860 she published a collection of her poems called *Poems before Congress*, which were political poems. Shortly after, her health deteriorated and she died on 29 June 1861. She is buried in Florence, Italy.

CHALLENGE > >

Research Robert Browning and write a summary of the type of poetry he wrote and the type of man he probably was. Then, based on the opinions you have formed of both poets, imagine you are Elizabeth Barrett and draft the speech she might make to her father begging him to allow her to marry Robert.

Sonnets

The sonnet originated in Italy in the 12th and 13th centuries and has become the most popular and enduring form of English verse. The best-known Italian writers of sonnets were Dante and Petrarch.

The word 'sonnet' comes from an Italian word meaning 'little song'. Since the 13th century, the term 'sonnet' has come to mean a poem of 14 lines that follows a strict rhyme scheme. The conventions associated with the sonnet have evolved over its history. Writers of sonnets are known as 'sonneteers'.

CHALLENGE > >

Research other sonneteers and come up with a list of ten famous sonneteers spanning the year 1500 to the present day. Try to identify the most famous sonnet that each wrote.

Extending

3.6 'Upon Westminster Bridge'

★ William Wordsworth

★ Wordsworth was born in the Lake District in 1770 and grew up in the countryside. He went to Cambridge University and became a great thinker – a philosopher, idealist, political activist and poet. He went to live in France during the French Revolution and admired the cause, fighting for equality and abolishing the gap between rich and poor.

Wordsworth is perhaps the most well-known Romantic poet and his poem (right) about daffodils is one of the most famous poems in English literature.

I wandered lonely as a cloud
That floats on high o'er vales and hills,
When all at once I saw a crowd,
A host, of golden daffodils;
Beside the lake, beneath the trees,
Fluttering and dancing in the breeze.

CHALLENGE >>>

1 Sketch the scene that this poem communicates to you – use the colour that you see in your mind as you create the image.
2 These lines suggest the poet is alone but what is his mood?
3 Although, of course, the daffodils are rooted to the ground, what is their mood and how are they able to express it?
4 For the poet, there is something joyous about suddenly coming upon the daffodils. Pick out the words that tell us this.

Settings in Romantic poetry

The Romantic poets were sensitive to scenes showing the power of nature and also the simplicity of a rural lifestyle. Paintings from the time often reflect this. The abbey pictured below is a beautiful and imposing building. It inspired this famous painting by Turner and an equally famous poem by Wordsworth.

◀ 'Tintern Abbey' by J. M. W. Turner, 1794

CHALLENGE >>>

1 Study the painting of Tintern Abbey (below left) and think about how the artist has captured the power and nature of the building and its surroundings.
> Describe the light and the way it falls into the ruin.
> Describe the surrounding landscape.
2 Now write a poem (or description) setting the scene in the painting and capturing the mood of the occasion.

3.7 'Mariana'

★ Alfred, Lord Tennyson

★ Tennyson was born in 1809. He is often considered to be the main representative of the Victorian age in poetry. Queen Victoria appointed Tennyson as Poet Laureate in 1850, replacing Wordsworth in the role. As Poet Laureate, he wrote poems to celebrate occasions of national importance and to honour the royal family.

★ Tennyson began to write poetry when he was young, in the style of Lord Byron, one of the Romantic poets. In 1830, he published *Poems, Chiefly Lyrical*, which included the popular 'Mariana'.

★ Tennyson continued to write poetry for many years and in the 1870s he wrote several plays. In 1884, he was made a baron. He died eight years later, on 6 October 1892, and is buried in Poets' Corner in Westminster Abbey.

▲ 'Mariana in the Moated Grange' by Millais

CHALLENGE >>>

1 Write your own poem which creates a setting of solitude and loneliness, just as the image above does. Start with a sketch and then write a poem to accompany it, trying to use a regular rhyme and rhythm as does Tennyson.

2 In pairs, discuss the poems you have written on solitude and explore their emotional effects and how they were achieved. Suggest possible improvements to each other's poems.

Victorian poetry

This term is used for poetry written during Queen Victoria's reign (1837–1901), during which poetry was highly thought of, along with other forms of writing. The sonnet was a popular form in Victorian poetry, such as in the work of Elizabeth Barrett Browning.

The Victorian era was a time of great change in science, religion, politics, art and literature. The Industrial Revolution had brought about important developments in science and technology, but it also created some serious social problems.

CHALLENGE >>>

Find out who the other important Victorian writers were and make a timeline with the names of important works on it. You could choose to concentrate on Victorian poetry, novels or plays. Copy the timeline below onto a large piece of paper.

1837
Victoria becomes Queen

1901
Queen Victoria dies

▲ Queen Victoria with her husband Prince Albert and some of their children

Extending

3.8 'Half-caste'

★ John Agard

- ★ John Agard was born on 21 June 1949 in British Guiana (now Guyana). He is a playwright, poet, short-story and children's writer. He worked for the *Guyana Sunday Chronicle* newspaper as sub-editor and feature writer before moving to England in 1977, when he took a job travelling to schools throughout the UK to promote a better understanding of Caribbean culture.
- ★ In 1993, he was appointed Writer in Residence at the South Bank Centre, London, and became Poet in Residence at the BBC in London. He won the Paul Hamlyn Award for Poetry in 1997 and has travelled extensively throughout the world performing his poetry.

★ Grace Nichols

- ★ John Agard is married to the poet Grace Nichols, who was also born in Guyana. She worked as a teacher and journalist and spent time in some of the most remote areas of Guyana. This was a period that influenced her writings and started up a strong interest in Guyanese folktales, Amerindian myths and the South American civilisations of the Aztec and Inca. She, also, has lived in the UK since 1977.
- ★ Grace Nichols is famous for her poem 'Island Man', which tells the story of a Caribbean man living in London. Every morning when he wakes up, he hears in his head the sound of the sea back home. She uses rhythm to make the poem feel like a reggae song and we can feel the way the island man strides along as we read the poem.

CHALLENGE > >

1 Write your own poem which uses an accent and/or a dialect, just as 'Half-caste' does. You can write the words phonetically (as they sound).
2 Do you know any dialect expressions? Write them down in one column and say what they mean in standard English in another column.
3 Do the same for the following proverbs, which are in a Guyanese dialect. Use your imagination to interpret them.
> Tongue nah gat teeth but he ah bite fuh true.
> The looks ah de pudding is not de taste.
> When coconut fall down from tree he can't fasten back.

▲ The poets John Agard and Grace Nichols

CHALLENGE > >

Write your own poem about what you hear in your head and what you think (or dream) of as you wake up every morning. Try to use a local accent or dialect, for example West Country, Cockney, Geordie or Scouse, and spell the words phonetically, i.e. as they sound.

3.9 'Human Beings'

★ Adrian Mitchell

★ Adrian Mitchell was born in 1932 and studied at Oxford University. He worked first of all as a reporter on various newspapers, but then moved into writing novels and poetry.

★ He is the author of four novels and has also written many poems and plays for adults and children. His collection of poetry entitled *Daft as a Doughnut* (2004) was chosen by the Poetry Book Society as the year's best single author collection of children's poems. He has written three storybooks about Baron Münchhausen and adaptations of well-known tales such as Hans Christian Andersen's *The Ugly Duckling*.

CHALLENGE >>

1 Find and read Adrian Mitchell's poem called 'Playground', which was written during the invasion of Iraq in 2003.
2 Make a list of the ways in which this poem is different from many poems.
3 Why do you think it is set out the way it is?
4 Discuss what the poem means to you, and how you might tell from it that Adrian Mitchell is a **pacificist**. If you have forgotten what this word means, look back to page 24.

Adrian Mitchell's ideas about poetry

Adrian Mitchell believes in writing poetry that is interesting, but is also accessible to as many people as possible. He thinks that 'Most people ignore most poetry because most poetry ignores most people.' His own poems – like 'Human Beings' – deal with recognisable subjects in clear, modern language. He often uses rhythms drawn from pop music in his poetry.

CHALLENGE >>

1 Write your own poem using the rhythm of your favourite pop song, on a subject of your choice. How about:
  > The life of young people today?
  > New technologies?
  > What you should and shouldn't wear this year?
  You might like to write it in an appropriate shape, as Adrian Mitchell does.
2 In pairs, discuss the poems you have just written and try to improve them.

▲ Poetry isn't just for you!

3.10 Creative response

Anglo-Saxon poetry

The poetry written by the Anglo-Saxons is usually referred to as 'Old English' poetry and was written between the mid-5th century and 1066 (the year of Norman Conquest). As most people could not read or write in those days, most of the poetry was passed on orally (by word of mouth).

Most Old English poets did not record their names, and the few that we are certain of today are Caedmon, Bede, Alfred and Cynewulf. Caedmon is the best known, and is considered to be the father of Old English poetry. He lived at the Abbey of Whitby in Northumbria in the 7th century.

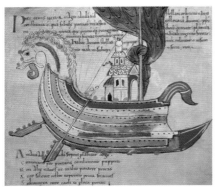

▲ An Anglo-Saxon manuscript.

★ Anglo-Saxon people

★ The Anglo-Saxons were the people who lived in Great Britain from around AD 450 to 1066, which was the year of the Norman invasion. They spoke Germanic dialects, which eventually merged together into what we call Old English, but it actually sounds very much like German. The Anglo-Saxons were from three different tribes: the Angles, the Saxons and the Jutes.

CHALLENGE > >

Research Anglo-Saxon poetry and find out what sort of things the poems were about and what their titles were. You are bound to come upon references to 'Beowulf'. What is this poem about and why is it so important?

CHALLENGE > >

1 Research other influences on the English language. What other languages influenced the language we speak today?
2 An etymological dictionary is one which tells you the origins of words. Use this kind of dictionary to discover the origins of the key words of the following passage.

I like to go to the theatre to see all kinds of plays and concerts. My favourite types are musicals and operas. Unfortunately, you are not allowed to take photographs inside the auditorium, but you can normally buy a video after the performance. I also like to purchase a programme and other souvenirs to remind me of the show I have seen.

4.1 Exploring sound and structuring stories

Thinking about narrative structure

Most stories or narratives can be divided into five sections:

- the opening
- the development
- the complication or further development
- the crisis or climax
- the resolution.

For example, if you were to analyse the structure of *Little Red Riding Hood*, it might look something like this:

The opening	Little Red Riding Hood lives on the edge of the forest with her mother.
The development	Her Grandma is sick, and Little Red Riding Hood has to take her a basket of food. The forest is very dangerous and her mother warns her not to stray from the path.
The complication or further development	She gets distracted by flowers on the way through the forest, and bumps into the Wolf. He tricks her into telling him where she is going. The Wolf races ahead, eats Grandma, puts on her nightdress and jumps in the bed.
The crisis or climax	Little Red Riding Hood arrives at Grandma's, and suddenly realises the horror of her situation as the Wolf jumps out of bed at her! She screams, and is rescued by the Woodcutter, who cuts off the Wolf's head, splits open the stomach, and pulls Grandma out alive!
The resolution	Grandma and Red Riding Hood are reunited, and Little Red Riding Hood promises always to do as her mother tells her in the future.

Choose another well-known story and create a table like the one below. Add the five sections from the one above in the left-hand column, in the second column write details about this stage of your chosen story and in the right-hand column think about what you would include in the soundtrack.

Story title:		
Stage of the story	**Details**	**Soundtrack**

CHALLENGE >>

Imagine you are turning *Little Red Riding Hood* into a film but the producer wants you to come up with ideas to give the characters, background and plot more modern relevance. How would you do it?

Extending

4.2 Exploring images and characters

In this lesson, you will have explored the ways we can often develop ideas about a character, by looking at some of the decisions a film-maker has made about:

- colours
- props
- gesture
- lighting
- costume
- body language
- setting
- facial features
- the position of a character.

For example, look at what might be suggested by the image on the right.
- Bright lighting lit from above suggests happiness and warmth.
- Lots of white in the setting and costumes suggests cleanliness, innocence and purity.
- Very clean kitchen suggests a happy and organised family.
- Mother and daughter look very alike – emphasising their closeness.
- Big mixing bowl suggests they are making a treat, like biscuits or a cake.
- Mother and daughter look directly in each other's eyes, emphasising their closeness.

The extract below is taken from *A Christmas Carol* by Charles Dickens, and introduces the character Scrooge.

> Scrooge! Hard and sharp as flint, and solitary as an oyster. The cold within him froze his old features, nipped his pointed nose. He carried his own low temperature always about with him.
>
> Nobody ever stopped him in the street to say, 'My dear Scrooge, how are you. When will you come to see me.' No beggars asked him to hand over a coin, no children asked him what it was o'clock. Even the blindmen's dogs appeared to know him; and when they saw him coming on, would tug their owners into doorways and up courts.
>
> But what did Scrooge care! It was the very thing he liked. To edge his way along the crowded paths of life, warning all human kind to keep its distance.
>
> Once upon a time – of all the good days in the year, on Christmas Eve – old Scrooge sat busy in his counting-house.

CHALLENGE >>

Imagine you are directing a film version of *A Christmas Carol*. The film will open with Scrooge in his office. Draw a sketch of the opening shot, and label it with notes about all the different elements listed at the top of this page. For example: What will the lighting be like? What details will you include in the setting? What props or costume will give clues about his character? Write a memo to the casting director telling him what type of actor to hire for the part of Scrooge.

Think of some of the opening scenes of famous films that you have seen. What makes a good beginning to a film? What should it try to achieve? Draw a table with three columns. Use the first to record the film's title, the second to describe the opening shots and the third to describe why they are effective or could be improved. Make notes on five or six films.

4.3 Exploring camera shots

In this lesson, you will have looked at the effects that different camera shots can have on an audience.

Directors choose camera shots for different reasons, for example:

	**Extreme close-up** Could be to show intense emotion or important details, e.g. the handle of a robber's gun sticking out of his pocket as he enters a bank.
	**Close-up** Could be to show a character's emotions: to show their feelings, character or reaction to someone else's words or actions.
	**Medium shot** Could be used to show the relationship between two characters in a shot.
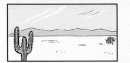	**Extreme wide shot** Could be to establish the scene, and tell the audience where they are, and to set the atmosphere.
	**Low-angle shot** Could be to make a character look intimidating or powerful.

CHALLENGE >>

Imagine you are directing a film version of Charles Dickens' *A Christmas Carol*. Look again at the extract on the previous page.

What kinds of shots might help to:
> Tell the audience where his office is?
> Create the right kind of mood right from the start?
> Show what other people think of Scrooge?
> Show what kind of person he is?
> Show what he thinks of other people?

CHALLENGE > >

You have decided to open the film *A Christmas Carol* with shots of Scrooge walking in the snow through the streets of London to his office. In order to better set the scene and to inform the audience of what kind of man Scrooge is, he is going to be muttering to himself a few sentences as he walks along. Write his brief speech on the right side of the page and on the left record the camera angles required to accompany his words.

Extending

4.4 The writer's/film-maker's viewpoint

Sometimes, when we read a novel or watch a film, it is easy to tell what the writer's attitude is towards a particular character or topic, but other times it is not so obvious.

CHALLENGE >>

Look at this extract from Charles Dickens' *Great Expectations*. The narrator, a young boy called Pip, meets a convict in the graveyard:

'Hold your noise!' cried a terrible voice, as a man started up from among the graves at the side of the church porch. 'Keep still, you little devil, or I'll cut your throat!'

A fearful man, all in coarse grey, with a great iron on his leg. A man with no hat, and with broken shoes, and with an old rag tied round his head. A man who had been soaked in water, and smothered in mud, and lamed by stones, and cut by flints, and stung by nettles, and torn by briars; who limped, and shivered, and glared and growled; and whose teeth chattered in his head as he seized me by the chin.

1 Identify the key words that the writer uses to convey his attitude to the character.
2 Imagine you are the young Pip being spoken to by the convict. Rewrite the extract as though the terrified boy had written it when confronted by this man.

CHALLENGE >>

Below is an extract from *Kensuke's Kingdom* by Michael Morpurgo. In no more than fifty words, describe the writer's attitude towards the character Kensuke.

He sat back on his haunches and tapped his chest.

'Kensuke. I, Kensuke. My island.' And he brought his hand down sharply like a chopper, separating the island in two. 'I, Kensuke. Here. You, boy. Here.' I was already in no doubt what he meant. Suddenly he was on his feet again waving me away with his stick.

'Go, boy. No fire. *Dameda*. No fire. You understand?'

I did not argue, but walked away at once. When, after a while, I dared to look back, he was kneeling down beside what was left of my fire, and scooping still more sand on to it.

Stella had stayed with him. I whistled for her. She came, but not at once. I could see that she was reluctant to leave him. She was behaving very oddly. Stella Artois had never taken kindly to strangers, never.

CHALLENGE >>

1 Having read this brief extract from *Kensuke's Kingdom*, what kind of book do you think it is? Is there a name for this kind of genre? Come up with ideas for what kind of setting the book has and what the plot might be about. Who or what might Stella Artois be?
2 When you have carefully considered these questions, check to see if you are correct by going to Michael Morpurgo's website.

www.michaelmorpurgo.org/
books_kensukes_kingdom

4.5 Exploring structure

In Lesson 1 of this unit, you looked at the importance of stages in the structure of a narrative for a reader. Now you are going to be looking at structure from the viewpoint of the writer, in preparation for your own creative writing.

CHALLENGE >>

1   Look at the following five images and order them so that they begin to form a narrative in your mind.

2   Now start to think about the five stages of your story. It could be that each of the images above represents a stage, but that is not necessarily the case. Thinking about your story, copy the grid below and add in the details in note form.

Stage	Narrative	Mood and pace
The opening		
The development		
The complication or further development		
The crisis or climax		
The resolution		

3   Begin the first paragraph of the story, either in the first or third person, setting the scene and trying to immediately grab the reader's interest. In the next lesson, you may want to change this slightly.

Extending

4.6 Creating your narrative

CHALLENGE >>

1 If your story is to take a real shape, the reader has to believe in your characters. Choose two characters from your story and decide on a name, age, their relationship to each other and three interesting facts about them. These facts don't need to feature in the story, but they will help you to make them realistic.

2 The last stage, and probably one of the most important ones, is to decide upon the narrator for the story:

> **first person** – 'I couldn't believe it was happening to **me**.'
> **second person** – '**You** couldn't believe it had happened to **you**.'
> **third person** – '**S/He** couldn't believe it was happening to **her/him**.'

If you decide on the first option, you must then consider which character is telling the story.

If you decide on one of the other two options, then you must decide from whose viewpoint they are seeing the narrative.

If you decide on the third person narrator, they could also be omniscient, which means they are looking at the story from everyone's view and can see everyone's thoughts.

Phew!

Under your grid, make a note of your narrator for this story.

Consider the advantages and disadvantages for this story of each possible narrative technique and briefly write them down in table form, before making your decision.

3 Now you are ready to begin to draft the story. Are you still happy with the opening you wrote in the last lesson? Does it need any alteration now you have firmly decided on the narrator? Think about the images and the story as a film to help you include the important details.

4.7 Storyboarding a section of your own film

A good storyboard should show us what the mood and atmosphere of a scene will be like. Have a look at the storyboard below, and think about what effect the finished film might have on an audience.

Composition: lush green rainforest, family wearing safari gear, sweating, and struggling through forest, dark shadows but beams of sunlight coming through the canopy, glints on Susie's blonde hair
Camera: cut to wide shot of family entering the thicker part of the rainforest, tracking shot as they climb over roots and branches
Sound: rainforest noise, distant chatter of walkers, calm music

Composition: walkers below looking ahead – not up – lush leaves partially block the view of them walking below
Camera: very high angle point-of-view long shot of walkers (POV monkey)
Sound: breathing noise and loud grunts, walker noise more quiet, unaware laughing and chatting

Composition: young cheeky-looking monkey with big eyes staring down and making faces
Camera: cut to extreme close-up of monkey's eyes, and zoom out to close-up of monkey's face
Sound: *Jaws*-style music that builds up to big raspberry noise made by monkey

Composition: girl has flushed red cheeks and messy hair – looks flustered and worried
Camera: cut to medium shot of girl searching around for source of noise, and then zoom to close-up of worried face
Sound: very quiet, cracks of twigs and odd rustling only, mysterious music

CHALLENGE >>

1 What effect does the tracking shot have in the first shot, rather than a still camera that the actors walk past?
2 Why do you think that the film-maker has chosen a point-of-view shot for the second shot, rather than showing us the monkey?
3 What do you think the effect of the breathing noise might be?
4 Why do you think the film-maker has chosen to follow this with an extreme close-up of the monkey's eyes?
5 What is the effect of the music and sound effects in the third shot? How does it affect the mood of the scene?

CHALLENGE >>

1 What do you think will happen next? Create the next three shots in this short sequence.
2 Briefly sketch out how you see the story developing, under the headings: The development, The complication or further development, The crisis or climax and The resolution.

Extending

4.8 Translating from film into written text

1 Think about this image from the film *Bush Bikes* and where it comes in the narrative.

2 From the jumble of words, phrases and ideas below, make a note of the ones that are most relevant to this image.

happy	cautious	excited	worried	jealous

smells   sights   feelings   sounds   tastes

long sentences   lots of commas in a list   short snappy sentences

ellipsis (…)   exclamation mark   questions

close-up   medium shot   long shot   medium long shot   extreme close-up

first person narrator   second person narrator   third person narrator

3 Write a brief description of what this image suggests and which aspects of the film it conveys to you.

4 Having seen the film *Bush Bikes*, write a brief review of it, bringing out its themes and how they are put across, and giving your opinion of its effectiveness.

4.9 Writing a section of your film

CHALLENGE >>

1 One important skill to learn when writing a narrative is how to show the passage of time. Think about how long *Bush Bikes* lasts as a film (5 minutes) and in real time (about 8 hours).

When do the big shifts in time occur in *Bush Bikes*? Make a note in the first two columns of a table like the one below. How long do you estimate each would take in real time?

Time shift	Estimated real time	Technique(s) used and reasons why
The boys look in the bike shop window – about 10 seconds of film.	15 minutes	• Lots of frames held for only a second on the screen to build the excitement and show how much there is to see in the shop. • Changing viewpoint looking at boys to seeing what they are seeing. • Fast-paced music with a clear beat to show their excitement.

2 Now think about how the film-maker manages the shift(s) in time, and make a note of the techniques they have used.
3 Look at your own narrative plan for your story. Where are the shifts in time? How long do they cover? Make a note on your story plan.
4 Now it is time to think about how you are going to show these transitions. Order these ideas from the shortest to the longest:

Order	Shifts in time
	As the twins grew older, they began to grow apart …
	French, Maths, Geography – in no time the bell went for lunch …
	Suddenly …
	Over the rest of the holiday, things didn't get any better …
	As day turned to night …

5 Now look at your own story and consider how to manage the transitions in time. Make a note of some ideas on your plan.
6 There are other types of transitions you can consider:
   > **Transitions in place:**
   'Over in the zoo, they had no idea of the growing problem …'
   > **Transitions in narrator:**
   'Without a word, he turned away … I had no idea where I would go as I walked away that September evening.'

Add any ideas for other transitions or shifts to your plan.

CHALLENGE >>

We all know that the last lesson on Friday afternoon, for example, seems endless, whilst the party later simply flies by. Discuss how shifting the time can apparently make it slow down or speed up.

Extending

4.10 Analysing narrative writing

Hopefully, if you have done a good job of 'translating' your storyboard from film into writing, then you will have created a really strong sense of mood and pace. It is useful for you to be able to explain how you have done this.

Below is an extract from a piece of narrative writing a student has written. A couple of the features have been picked out.

▶ Onomatopoeia used to recreate the sounds of the jungle for the reader

▶ The writer withholds information – we don't know what her fears are and this adds to the tense mood

Suddenly, without any warning, Susie's worst fears were realised. There was a tremendous thrashing and crashing – a rustling of leaves and twigs in the canopy, and it erupted out of the trees. Whooping, wailing and arms flailing, the sleek grey gibbon flew towards her. Its mouth was fixed in a wild grin of glee and menace. It landed on the ground before her … paused for as short moment, and then took off again.

CHALLENGE >>

Looking at your own piece of writing, text mark how you have created a strong mood and pace.

When analysing writing, it is important to develop your ideas:

Point	Choose one idea that answers the question.	The writer uses lots of onomatopoeia to create a chaotic and dramatic mood in the jungle.
Evidence	Choose one line that best demonstrates your point.	For example, she writes about the 'thrashing and crashing' and rustling' in the canopy.
Explanation	Explain how this line creates a strong mood and/or pace.	The sounds of these words recreate what it must have felt and sounded like for Susie, and make it sound like a huge commotion.

CHALLENGE >>

> What is your own worst fear? Write two paragraphs, similar to those in the extract, beginning the first with: 'Suddenly, my worst fear was realised …'.

5.1 Rules, rules, rules

A unit of work on speaking and listening assumes that we can all speak and hear, but of course not everyone can. People may be deaf, blind or unable to speak properly, but there are still lots of ways for them to communicate. How many can you think of?

You may have heard of Guide Dogs for the Blind, but did you know that about one in seven people has a hearing problem in the UK, and that there are also Hearing Dogs for the Deaf? You can find out more about these dogs at http://www.hearingdogs.org.uk/.

Imagine you are a hearing dog and describe your owner and some of the typical ways you help him or her. Write a couple of paragraphs.

CHALLENGE >>

Find out what this symbol is and make a list of the places that you might see it.

CHALLENGE >>

Have a look at the finger alphabet for the deaf. See if you can learn to tell someone who is deaf what your name is.

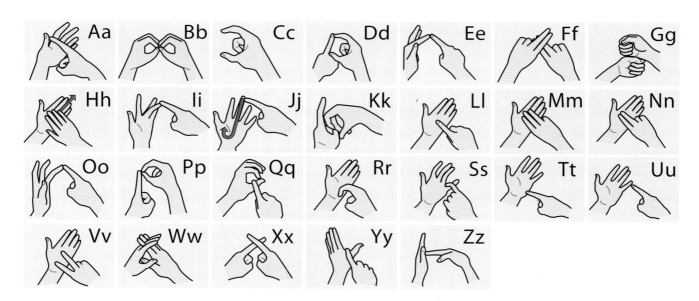

CHALLENGE >>

Bearing in mind there are so many people who suffer from hearing problems, make out a case that sign language should be taught in schools to all pupils. Write notes that you could turn into a speech.

5.2 Home versus school

Homeschooling

School became compulsory in the 19th century. Until then most education happened at home and only a few people used tutors or sent children to school. Nowadays, most children in developed nations attend school.

Homeschooling is when parents and carers choose to educate children at home – often doing the teaching themselves – rather than sending children to school. People choose homeschooling today when they wish to provide an education or an environment that they believe is not available in schools.

CHALLENGE >>

With your partner, role play a discussion between two pupils – one school educated and the other home educated – both trying to convince each other of the benefits of their educational system.

★ The Education Act

- ★ The Education Act of 1870 began the national system of state education – children between the ages of 5 and 13 had to go to elementary school.
- ★ The country was divided into school districts, each of which ensured that they provided schools for all the children aged 5–13.
- ★ Schools could charge up to 9d (4p) a week. School Boards could pay the fees if the parents were unable to do so.
- ★ Education became effectively free with the passing of the 1891 Education Act.
- ★ The School Board could appoint one of the School Attendance Officers or 'Board Men' to find children who played truant. These officers became a frightening figure in the minds of young schoolchildren.

Worldwide education today

- There are about 115 million children worldwide who can't go to school because of poverty, war, child labour, or because they have no school in their district or no birth certificate.
- Almost one in five of all children under 11 in the world are not in school.
- Less developed countries have the biggest problems: more than a third of out-of-school children live in South Asia.
- In Somalia, nine out of ten children do not go to school.

CHALLENGE >>

Research a less developed country and find out why children in that country find attending school so hard, or impossible. Suggest ways in which people in more advanced countries can help to provide schools for those less fortunate.

5.3 The big debate

Homeschooling – the debate

Here are some famous opinions about education that will help you to contribute to the debate today.

'All men who have turned out worth anything have had the chief hand in their own education.' – Sir Walter Scott

'A child cannot be taught by anyone who despises him.' – James Baldwin

'Bless me, what *do* they teach them at these schools?' – C. S. Lewis, *The Lion, the Witch and the Wardrobe*

'Education is an admirable thing, but it is well to remember from time to time that nothing that is worth knowing can be taught.' – Oscar Wilde

'For me, home education has been a terrific journey away from static forms of learning, institutional hoops to jump through, forms to please others, and a journey into a magical world of wonder and discovery. Not relaxing, but certainly an exciting process.' – Val, California, homeschool mum

'How is it that little children are so intelligent and men so stupid? It must be education that does it.' – Alexandre Dumas

'I suppose it is because nearly all children go to school nowadays and have things arranged for them that they seem so forlornly unable to produce their own ideas.' – Agatha Christie

'It is possible to store the mind with a million facts and still be entirely uneducated.' – Alec Bourne

'A little learning is a dangerous thing; drink of it deeply, or taste it not, for shallow thoughts intoxicate the brain, and drinking deeply sobers us again.' – Alexander Pope

'An investment in knowledge always pays the best interest.' – Benjamin Franklin (1706–1790), American Founding Father and scientist

'Earth and sky, woods and fields, lakes and rivers, the mountain and the sea, are excellent schoolmasters, and teach some of us more than we can ever learn from books.' – John Lubbock

'I have never let my schooling interfere with my education.' – Mark Twain

▲ The old days

CHALLENGE >>

Pick out four or five of the expressions on the left and write them in one column. In a second column explain briefly what they really mean and in the third say why you agree or disagree with them.

CHALLENGE >>

Research how schooling has changed in this country over the last 100 years and write a 200-word item for your own personal blog outlining your findings and reactions.

5.4 Airs and graces

◀ How it was back then

★ Radio

★ During the 1920s, the power of radio advertising first became obvious. Radios were the new technology of the time, much like the internet today, and were the new way of reaching large numbers of people at one time. This was very powerful.

★ Advertising was an important way for broadcasters to help fund their programming. Radio was an especially successful way to reach audiences in the 1920s – most families had access to a radio during this time.

★ The radio was the main source of entertainment. It broadcast dramas, the news and other information.

★ The term 'soap opera' as we know it came into being as soap manufacturers sponsored domestic radio dramas in return for frequent plugs (mentions) for their product.

CHALLENGE > >

1 Before the ages of television and the computer, radio provided a great deal of family entertainment. Imagine this is still the case and you are in charge of one day's programming, from 9am until 8pm. Devise a schedule for that day which would appeal to a typical modern family.

2 Design a page for the day you are in charge of programming for the *Radio Times*. Include the running order and some brief description of each programme.

Radio advertising today

Today, the amount of money spent on radio campaigns is relatively small. In general, local businesses advertise on their local radio station. National advertising, across the whole country, takes place on television or in newspapers and magazines. The money spent advertising in these media is far greater than that spent on advertising on the radio.

In the future, it will not be many years before the internet challenges all these media in terms of successful advertising.

▲ The way ahead

5.5 Global gamble

Global travel

Flying abroad for pleasure has been a growth industry for 40 years or more. Flights to far-flung destinations like Australia have become common and fashionable. Aviation fuel is relatively damaging to the environment, with its carbon dioxide and other emissions.

★ Friends of the Earth

- ★ Many pressure groups have taken action against air travel by speaking out.
- ★ One of these is Friends of the Earth.
- ★ They say that 'air transport is the fastest-growing emitter of greenhouse gases and it causes a range of other significant environmental impacts, including noise, air pollution, land take and destruction of wildlife habitats'.

★ Responsible Travel

- ★ Even with over one billion people taking flights every year, there are many who believe that it is possible to fly responsibly.
- ★ One such company is called Responsible Travel.
- ★ They say that 'nearly everything that we do in our lives contributes to CO_2 emissions and global warming. Flying is no exception and, although currently a relatively small source of emissions (less than 5% of the total and far less than that created by our houses or the clothes we buy), it is the fastest growing of all. There is no doubt that we must all fly significantly less than we do now, but there is still a case for responsible travel'.

▲ Would you give up flying?

CHALLENGE >>

Draw up a chart listing all the benefits that there are for people travelling widely on holiday. List in a second column the environmental downside to each benefit.

CHALLENGE >>

Go on Friends of the Earth's website and look at the section on climate change to collect information to enable you to make a fact sheet about the dangers of greenhouse gases.

responsibletravel.com
holidays that give the world a break

5.6 I have a dream

Martin Luther King was born on 15 January 1929 in Atlanta, Georgia, in America. He was originally named Michael, but became Martin later. He became Dr Martin Luther King in 1955 after studying Theology at Boston University. His father was a Baptist minister and his mother a schoolteacher.

He fought for equal rights for all people, regardless of their race or colour. He gave his famous 'I have a dream' speech in 1963 and was given the Nobel Peace Prize in 1964. King had many enemies in people who didn't want equality for all races, and was assassinated on 4 April 1968.

Yes, if you want to say that I was a drum major. Say that I was a drum major for justice. Say that I was a drum major for peace. Say that I was a drum major for righteousness. And all of the other shallow things will not matter. I won't have any money to leave behind. I won't have the fine and luxurious things in life to leave behind. But I just want to leave a committed life behind. And that's all I want to say. If I can help somebody as I pass along, if I can cheer somebody with a word or song, if I can show somebody he is travelling wrong, then my living will not be in vain.'

★ Rosa Parks

- ★ One of the people Martin Luther King met was Rosa Parks.
- ★ Rosa Parks became famous because, on 1 December 1955, she refused (as a black woman) to give up her seat to a white man on her local bus.
- ★ She was arrested, and this incident became an important moment in the fight for racial equality in America.

CHALLENGE >>

Write Rosa Parks' diary entry for the day she refused to give up her seat to a white man. In about a hundred words, try to capture what motivated her and her hopes and fears for the future.

CHALLENGE > >

1 The 'I have a dream' speech is the most famous of Martin Luther King's speeches. Look at the text on the left, from another speech, to see some of the other things he had to say. Discuss the ways in which this speech is able to make such an impact.

2 Write a short speech like this which aims to alert people to something in society you consider wrong and which will help to improve the situation.

5.7 *Just a Minute*

You may have heard the expression 'to get on your soap box'. It is used to describe someone when they are being forceful, talking passionately about a subject they feel strongly about.

In order to raise themselves up so that an audience could see and hear them better, speakers used to stand on a packing case originally used to transport soap. This method of having a quick and temporary stage is still used today. Look at the picture below of a speaker in Hyde Park, London.

Today we can use computer blogs to tell people what we think. The term 'blog' is a blend. It comes from merging the words 'web' and 'log'!

★ Speaker's Corner

- ★ Speaker's Corner is in Hyde Park, London, and is also called Hyde Park Corner.
- ★ It is a place where anyone can go and tell the world their views.
- ★ The tradition of using this area of the park began in 1855, when the Government brought in the Sunday Trading Bill, which prevented buying and selling on a Sunday. As Sunday was the only day most people had off from work, it was their only opportunity to shop for essentials.
- ★ People protested in Hyde Park and the park has been used ever since as a place for people to give others their views.

Extending

5.8 It's my life

Lots of artists have thought about the words 'It's my life …' Have a look at some of the things they have written as a result.

This ain't a song for the broken-hearted
A silent prayer for the faith-departed
I ain't gonna be just a face in the crowd
You're gonna hear my voice
When I shout it out loud

It's my life
It's now or never
I ain't gonna live forever
I just want to live while I'm alive

It's my life by Jon Bon Jovi

Here is another song called *It's my life*. It was originally written by the band Talk Talk but No Doubt, who had Gwen Stefani in their line-up, recorded a cover version.

Funny how I find myself
In love with you
If I could buy my reasoning
I would pay to lose
One half won't do
I've asked myself how much do you
Commit yourself?
It's my life
Don't you forget
It's my life
It never ends
Funny how I blind myself
I never knew
If I was sometimes played upon
Afraid to lose
I'd tell myself what good you do
Convince myself
It's my life
Don't you forget
It's my life
It never ends
I've asked myself how
much do you
Commit yourself?
It's my life
Don't you forget
It's my life
Caught in the crowd
It never ends.

It's my life by Talk Talk

CHALLENGE >>

1 What written features do you notice in the lyrics on this page?
2 What similar techniques could you use?
3 Using similar techniques,
   > Either:
     Write your own lyrics about an aspect of your life or feelings.
   > Or:
     Imagine you are a famous rock star whose popularity is fading – and explain, in a song, your feelings now that you can see you are on your way out.

5.9 I'm in charge

CHALLENGE >>

Look at the use of repetition in Winston Churchill's famous 'Beaches' speech from World War II. Have a go at reading it aloud.

Insert one more phrase into it that you think Churchill might have written.

We shall go on to the end, we shall fight in France, we shall fight on the seas and oceans, we shall fight with growing confidence and growing strength in the air, we shall defend our Island, whatever the cost may be, we shall fight on the beaches, we shall fight on the landing grounds, we shall fight in the fields and in the streets, we shall fight in the hills; we shall never surrender...

This is an extract from Gordon Brown's acceptance speech when he became British Prime Minister in 2007.

To those who feel the political system doesn't listen and doesn't care;

To those who feel powerless and have lost faith;

To those who feel Westminster is a distant place and politics simply a spectator sport;

I will strive to earn your trust. To earn your trust not just in foreign policy but earn your trust in our schools, in our hospitals, in our public services, and to respond to your concerns.

CHALLENGE >>

Look at the number of times he uses the 'rule of three'. This is a very clever speech. Gordon Brown uses 'To those who feel …' three times, and we know the 'rule of three' is a powerful and effective way of speaking and writing. So that he doesn't upset anyone, he makes no comment about whether he thinks they are **right** to feel this way!

He balances each of the first three sentences around the word 'and'. He uses the word 'trust' three times, giving three examples of where there needs to be trust – schools, hospitals and public services. Brown uses the pronouns 'your' and 'our' to make it seem as if there is a link between him and the audience.

Try to use similar techniques in your own work.

CHALLENGE > >

Look back at the work you did in Lesson 7, (page 47), when writing notes for a famous person's speech. Now script the opening paragraph, using three sentences that have an accumulative effect like the examples above. Make the paragraph as polished and as powerful as you can.

Extending

5.10 Student choice

We have already learned some of the techniques that go into making effective speeches – especially if we want to persuade our audience. Look at the other techniques below, some of which you will already know, and try them out in your work.

- **Alliteration** (repetition of initial consonant sounds) – 'A *short, sharp, shock!*'
- **Assonance** (repetition of vowel sounds) – 'Let the *fine* fit the crime.'
- **Balance** – 'Every cloud has a silver lining.'

EVERY CLOUD HAS A SILVER LINING

CHALLENGE >>

Refer back to the speech you began working on in Lesson 7, (page 47) and continued in the last lesson.

> Complete the speech, using some of the techniques explained on this page.
> When you have finished, underline the different techniques you have used and colour code them.

- **Contrast** (often opposites) – 'good versus evil', 'night and day' …
- **Description** (often using metaphor, simile and personification) – 'Whilst we wait, a blanket of fear smothers the land like fog on a motorway.'
- **Emotive language** (words to create an emotion in the listener) – 'They are *cold, lonely* and *terrified*.'
- **Hyperbole** (exaggerating to create an effect) – *Millions* of people…
- **Rhetorical questions** (those that don't require an answer) – 'Would you like to live in the sewers like vermin?'

6.1 Gathering information

Here is an example of an informative text on how to look after your pet. It is clearly trying to give as much information about pet care as possible to its readers. It aims to stop pets being neglected by their owners or to prevent people buying a pet without thinking about how much care it will need.

RSPCA pet care: Rabbits

Rabbits are difficult to look after. They need lots of space, and large homes that can be expensive to create. Before getting any pet, think very hard about whether you can provide everything it needs.

WHAT DO RABBITS NEED?

- Companionship – to be with other rabbits or humans. The widespread practice of keeping rabbits and guinea pigs together is not recommended.
- A mixed diet of grass, rabbit pellets, apples, carrots, dandelions and a good quantity of hay.
- A constant supply of fresh, clean drinking water in a drip-feed bottle with metal spout.
- A large weatherproof home off the ground, out of direct sunlight and strong winds. Move to an indoor area or porch in cold weather – many homes sold in pet shops are too small.
- A separate covered sleeping area for each animal.
- A clean layer of wood shavings and plenty of hay or shredded paper for bedding.
- Daily exercise in a large, safe grassy area.
- Rabbits burrow, so ensure the enclosure is sunk into the ground, escape-proof and safe from predators.
- Their home must be cleaned every day and bedding needs to be changed weekly.
- A gnawing block to wear down long teeth.
- To be brushed every day if they have a long coat.
- To be neutered at any early age. Ask your vet.
- Injections to prevent serious diseases.
- To be taken to a vet if they are ill or injured.
- To be looked after when you are on holiday.

CHALLENGE >>

1 Produce your own informative text on looking after a pet of your choice. Remember you will need to research information about the animal first, so that whoever reads your pet care information considers the needs of that animal carefully.
2 Look at your text with a partner and consider its strengths and weaknesses as a piece of information.
   > Does it do what you intended?
   > Is all the information presented factually correct?
   > Could any parts of it be misinterpreted?
   > How could you improve it and what illustrative material could you add?

6.2 Language and presentation – part 1

Match up these media terms and techniques that are used in adverts, with their explanations.

Media terms and techniques	Explanations
1 Background	**a** A picture where the camera is a little bit back from the subject – this is good for showing more of the body.
2 Long shot	**b** What can be seen at the front of the advert.
3 Medium shot	**c** What is being sold by the advertising company.
4 Foreground	**d** A picture where the camera is very near to the subject – this is good for showing faces.
5 Close-up	**e** The overall idea behind an advert or campaign.
6 Slogan	**f** The use of colour in an image which can be used for certain effects.
7 Colour image	**g** Who the advert is aimed at.
8 Product	**h** A catchphrase for a brand which is memorable.
9 Target audience	**i** What can be seen behind the main focus of the advert.
10 Concept	**j** A picture where the camera is quite a distance from the subject – this is good for showing group pictures and including a lot of the background.

1 Find an advert in a newspaper or a magazine which uses an image to represent the product it is selling. Consider how the choice of image, layout and presentation contribute to the effective advertising of the product. In particular, look at:
> the way the photograph, picture or diagram has been used
> the use of a headline, slogan or caption
> any other features of layout and design
2 From the choice of image and the product, who do you think the target audience is?

Answer:
1 i; 2 j; 3 a; 4 b; 5 d; 6 h; 7 f; 8 c; 9 g; 10 e.

6.3 Language and presentation – part 2

Adverts

Below is an advert for a computer. As you can see it uses a cat to promote the product. If you look carefully you will see the tail of a mouse in its mouth.

CHALLENGE >>>

1 How many of the media terms/techniques can you see being used within the advert?

2 Now analyse the advert using the following questions to help you.
   > What is the product being sold and who is the target audience?
   > What do you see on the advert? Describe it in detail.
   > What is effective about the choice of colour used?
   > What is the slogan and why is it effective?
   > How is the animal being presented?
   > Why was the animal chosen for that particular product? What is the purpose of using it?

3 Summarise why this advert is effective and how it is persuasive. Try to refer to the media terms as well within your response.

4 Imagine you are the executive of an advertising agency which has just produced this advert for a firm. Write a letter to the firm explaining how and why the advert is effective and will persuade people to buy their product.
   > Use media terms but make it clear what they mean if there is any doubt.
   > Explain exactly how the advert will appeal to the target audience.

The EPSON Stylus Photo 790. Catch every detail for just £110.

Don't be fooled by the innocent looks of the EPSON Stylus Photo 790, or the titchy price tag. Underneath it's a serious studio quality photo printer. An amazing 2880 cpi and 6 colour inks give stunning true photo print quality. Print on 4x6 and A4 media and you can have your photos without borders. And for immediate results, it prints at an amazing 7.8ppm black and white and 7.5ppm colour. It also comes with USB and Parallel interfaces for connection to PC and Mac.

All in all the EPSON Stylus Photo 790 is a pretty deceptive animal. For more information call 0800 220 546 or visit our website at www.epson.co.uk.

EPSON®

Extending

6.4 Planning a leaflet

The actress Lucy Davis is currently campaigning for PETA (People for the Ethical Treatment of Animals). She wants to stop Canadian black bears being killed so they can be used to make caps for the Queen's Guards. She has been quoted as saying:

> " It can take the entire hide of one bear to make just one guard's headpiece. Many of the bears are shot several times before they die, and some escape the hunters and bleed to death. When mother bears are killed, orphaned cubs are left behind to starve ... It's just for one hat. "

How many bears in books and ▶ films can you think of?

★ Acronyms and abbreviations

★ An acronym is a word formed by the initial letters of other words, in the way that 'PETA' is an acronym for 'People for the Ethical Treatment of Animals'. Simple abbreviations are used for many organisations. Do you know what the letters in these other animal organisations stand for?
- RSPCA
- RSPB
- WWF

CHALLENGE > >

Write a letter to the Minister for Animal Welfare asking him to put an end to the killing of the Canadian black bear. Make out a strong and convincing case.

Did you know?

In the UK, approximately 200 animals are held captive in circuses, although there are strict animal welfare rules to make sure the animals are treated humanely. In some countries, it is standard practice to beat, shock and whip animals in order to make them repeatedly perform tricks that make no sense to them.

CHALLENGE > >

1 What is your own view of circuses? Discuss the question with a partner, one of you arguing for them and one against.
2 Plan and mock up a leaflet either persuading people to go to and support the circus or persuading people that circuses should be banned.

6.5 Writing a leaflet

Zoos

- The first public zoo was the Ménagerie du Jardin des Plantes, founded in Paris in 1794 for scientific and educational purposes.
- London Zoo was established in 1828.
- Throughout the 1970s, zoos began to make conservation one of their main concerns. The naturalist Gerald Durrell was one of the main campaigners.
- Many zoos now keep animals in enclosures that are like their natural habitats.
- Whipsnade Park in Bedfordshire was the first wild animal park to be opened (in 1931). It covers 2.4 square kilometres and is still one of Europe's largest wildlife conservational parks.
- The first public aquarium was opened in London Zoo in 1853.
- In 2005, the largest aquarium opened in Atlanta in the USA. It uses more than 36 million litres of marine and fresh water, and has more than 100,000 animals of 500 different species.

★ Methane gas

★ The biggest emitters of methane gas are cows! Farmers are currently trying to find a diet for their cows that will reduce the amount of gas they release.

CHALLENGE >>

1 Do you approve of zoos?
  - > What are the arguments for?
  - > What are the arguments against?
  - > Make a 'For' and 'Against' table about zoos.
2 Now sketch out an advert for a zoo that is in your area. Pick a suitable slogan.

Our environment

There are many threats to our environment today:

- **global warming:** rising temperatures, greenhouse gases, destruction of the ozone layer, glaciers melting due to changing climates all over the world
- **pollution:** acid rain, oil spills, pesticides and chemicals
- **destruction of animal habitats:** deforestation, damage to coral reefs, an increase in the human population.

CHALLENGE >>

1 What is the potential impact on wildlife of the environmental problems on the left? Make a list of the five most damaging changes that are likely to occur and explain in detail what the effects are likely to be.
2 Using the techniques you have learnt in your class lessons, plan and write up a persuasive leaflet on one of these subjects:
  - > The effect of the changes to the environment on wildlife.
  - > Either the advantages of zoos, or the disadvantages of zoos.
  - > Either the advantages of circuses, or the disadvantages of circuses.

6.6 Animals in the media

Read this transcript from the voice-over for a film trailer of *Wallace and Gromit: The Curse of the Were-Rabbit*.

They've mesmerised audiences.
They've delighted millions.
Now Wallace and Gromit in their first thrilling motion picture
The gardens of England lie in danger,
from a terror so fierce –
it will petrify your parsnips
curdle your carrots,
and chill you to the marrow.
Our only hope is Wallace and Gromit!

Wallace and Gromit: The Curse of the Were-Rabbit!

CHALLENGE >>

Write a story which could be turned into a new film involving an animal that becomes a superhero, and then storyboard a trailer for it. Use a grid like the one below. Draw your images down the left and write the voice-over transcripts alongside.

Images	Voice-over transcripts

HAVING A BALL ...
THE SOCCER STAR THEY USED TO CALL 'CRAZY HORSE'

by David Wilkes

With skills like this, we'll soon be seeing him on *Match of the Neigh*.

Hoofing an oversized ball effortlessly down the field is Kariba, the horse world's very own Stanley Matthews.

When it comes to soccer, the magnificent stallion is game for anything. He can take a scorching shot at goal, and he's no donkey in midfield, either – able to pass, dribble and even do a 'header' with his nose.

At one time, Kariba's life seemed destined to be one constant red card. He was so unruly that he regularly threw his riders and was considered unsafe.

However, all that changed when equine psychologist Emma Massingale discovered his passion for football and saw that playing it helped calm him down. 'We started by leading him to the ball with a rope and I rewarded him with a pat if he touched or kicked it,' said 25-year-old Miss Massingale, who rehabilitates dangerous mounts at her training school, Natural Equine, in Bradworthy, Devon.

'Horses naturally shy away from unusual, bright objects that move towards them, so that had to be overcome.

'Luckily, he is such a showoff that he took to it immediately and there was no looking back. He loves to learn new tricks and will parade around showing off his skills without any instruction.'

Miss Massingale – who has had Kariba for eight years – gained her skills in the Australian Outback, where she learned to understand the psyche of each individual horse. Three months ago, she tried the stallion with a football after watching a match with her fiancé Jeremy Colwill, 41.

As his confidence grew, 16-year-old Kariba began playing alone, and even invented his own moves.

▲ Just horsing about: The stallion was once so unruly he threw his riders.

'Using the ball gives him a sense of responsibility and focus, which allows him to develop a higher level of intelligence,' said Miss Massingale.

'He is problem-solving and accepting changing situations. It will make him smarter, keep him fit and he also quite literally seems to get a kick out of it.'

Meanwhile, several teams are said to be showing an interest in the star, including Steeds United, Foalham, Horsenal, Bolting Wanderers and Mountchester United.

CHALLENGE >>

1 Read the article above and make a list of as many features of a newspaper article as you can find.
2 Write your own newspaper article about an animal that has a special gift. Remember to include a catchy headline, facts, detail, direct quotes from people, a picture and a strong concluding paragraph.

Extending

6.8 Noah's Ark

Who am I?

▶ I live in the ocean.
I can smell one tiny drop of blood in 100 litres of water.
I have 3,000 teeth but no bones!
They call me Jaws – I have a bad reputation but I don't think it's fair.
Who am I?

▶ I am as tall as a man but walk on all fours.
My closest relation is a man but also my only enemy
You will only find me in Africa, but a famous family member once visited New York.
He was called King Kong.
Who am I?

▶ I carry my house on my back.
I am both male and female.
I cannot see but I can feel.
My slimy trail is so strong
I can move along a razor's edge without getting cut.
Who am I?

CHALLENGE >>

1 Write your own animal 'Who am I?' riddle using factual information about the animal. Discuss it with a partner to decide if it is too easy or too hard, or if it could be improved.

2 Choose an animal that you would like to write a poem about. Jot down some vivid, interesting words to describe:
  > shape
  > size
  > colour
  > movement
  > sound

3 Come up with some original similes or metaphors to describe any of the above features.

4 Describe what mood/tone is appropriate for a poem about your chosen animal.
  > What sorts of sounds will help you to create that mood? Harsh consonants? Short vowels? Soft consonants? Long vowels?
  > Try to use alliteration and/or assonance to help you create the right mood.

5 Use some of these ideas to help you write your poem.
  Remember: poems don't always have to rhyme!

6 Write out your completed poem and then use arrows and colour coding to highlight the features you have included.

▶ I am the biggest cat but you wouldn't want me to sit on your lap.
My saliva is an antiseptic – handy when I've wounded myself in the hunt for food.
Even if you shaved my fur off, you would still see my distinctive orange and black stripes!
Who am I?

▶ I have a trunk but not a suitcase.
I walk on my toes but you wouldn't want me to step on you!
I am the biggest animal on land but that doesn't stop humans killing me for my ivory.
I never forget.
Who am I?

6.9 Writing a speech

Animal speeches

The two speeches below are about equality and freedom for animals. Humans are the enemy in both.

Old Major's speech in *Animal Farm*

'My friends I do not think I will be with you for many days more. I've had a long life, and now it is my duty to pass onto you such as I understand of the nature of our lives.

Animalkind is born to a miserable, laborious and short existence. We are given only just enough food as will sustain the breath in our bodies and, when our usefulness has come to an end, we are slaughtered with hideous cruelty. And who, pray, is responsible for our suffering?
Man. Man is our enemy ...

Remove man, and the root cause of hunger and overwork is abolished forever. Remove man, and the produce of our labour will be our own. Remove man, and overnight we will become free and equal ...

We must never come to resemble man in any way, or engage in trade.

Amongst us animals there must be unity and comradeship. All animals are friends. All humans are enemies. Now, my friends, I will tell you about the end of my dream and the song that came to me. It's a song you must learn.

It's a song of justice and freedom.'

Chicken Run

It's all in your head. It's all in your head. Think, everyone, think. What haven't we tried yet? We haven't tried not trying to escape. Hmm. That might work. What about Edwina? How many more empty nests will it take? It wouldn't be empty if she'd spent more time laying. And less time escaping. So, laying eggs all your life, then getting plucked and roasted is good enough for you? It's a living.

The problem is the fences aren't just round the farm, they're up here in your heads. There is a better place out there. Somewhere beyond that hill. It has wide-open spaces and lots of trees. And grass.

Can you imagine that? Cool, green grass.
– Who feeds us? We feed ourselves.
– Where's the farm? There is no farm.
– Where does the farmer live? – There is no farmer.

Is he on holiday? He isn't anywhere. Don't you get it? There's no egg count, no farmers, no dogs and coops and keys, and no fences! In all my life, I've never heard such a fantastic load of tripe! Face the facts, ducks. The chances of us getting out of here are a million to one.

Then there's still a chance ...
Freedo-o-o-om!

CHALLENGE >>

1 In your class lessons, you have been working on writing a speech in favour of the animal you chose to board Noah's Ark. Write down a list of the persuasive techniques used in these speeches that you could use in your own speech and explain how they work. You should find examples of:
> personal pronouns
> repetition
> the rule of '3'
> emotive language
> powerful concluding statement

2 Make a list of what both speeches on this page have in common, using quotations to support your ideas.

Extending

6.10 Sink or swim

Read this extract from *The Hobbit*, where Bilbo fights the monstrous spider.

He was deep in thoughts of bacon and eggs and toast and butter when he felt something touch him. Something like a strong sticky string was against his left hand and when he tried to move he found that his legs were already wrapped in the same stuff, so that when he got up he fell over.

Then the great spider, who had been busy tying him up while he dozed, came from behind him and came at him. He could only see the thing's eyes, but he could feel its hairy legs as it struggled to wind its abominable threads round and round him. It was lucky that he had come to his senses in time. Soon he would not have been able to move at all. As it was, he had a desperate fight before he got free. He beat the creature off with his hands – it was trying to poison him to keep him quiet, as small spiders do to flies – until he remembered his sword and drew it out. Then the spider jumped back, and he had time to cut his legs loose. After that it was his turn to attack. The spider evidently was not used to things that carried such stings at their sides, or it would have hurried away quicker. Bilbo came at it before it could disappear and stuck it with his sword right in the eyes. Then it went mad, and leaped and danced and flung out its legs in horrible jerks, until he killed it with another stroke; and then he fell down and remembered nothing more for a long while.

CHALLENGE >>

1 Read the extract above and discuss with a partner how the writer has created tension in it.
  > Pick out words and phrases that are particularly effective.
  > What is our reaction to the spider's attempts to tie up Bilbo, to the way he deals with it and to its death?
2 Write a story where an important character battles with a fierce animal. Maybe it is a make-believe animal you create from your imagination or perhaps it is an animal that you fear already. It could be set in the past or in the future.

7.1 Fair is foul and foul is fair

★ Shakespeare

- ★ Shakespeare was born in 1564, probably on 23 April, and died in 1616 – also on 23 April.
- ★ He wrote 38 plays and more than 150 poems called sonnets.
- ★ He married Anne Hathaway on 27 November 1582.
- ★ Shakespeare 'disappeared' between 1585 and 1592, and it is thought that he may have been abroad as a spy.
- ★ Records show that Shakespeare wasn't always honest, hoarding grain when there was a shortage, and he was often accused of not paying his taxes!

▲ Anne Hathaway's cottage

Round about the cauldron go;
In the poison'd entrails throw.
Toad, that under cold stone
Days and nights has thirty-one
Swelter'd venum sleeping got.
Boil thou first i' the charmed pot

CHALLENGE >>

You probably have heard the name of Francis Bacon as a possible writer of Shakespeare's plays. Below are some of the arguments often used to suggest Bacon's authorship. Discuss with a partner which points you find the most and the least convincing:

1. Bacon was associated with many people who knew Shakespeare.
2. He claimed to be a 'concealed poet', i.e. to have kept secret the fact that he wrote poetry.
3. Like Shakespeare he had an enormous vocabulary and often made up new words.
4. Many of the expressions and metaphors used by Bacon are very similar to those found in the plays.
5. Bacon left a manuscript listing his works which included some of the plays.
6. Two people who both knew Shakespeare well, Thomas Greene and John Marston, both claimed that Bacon wrote some of his works.

The curse of *Macbeth*

Did you know that the play *Macbeth* is meant to be cursed? It is said that witches were so annoyed William Shakespeare used spells in the play that they cursed it. Lots of actors won't refer to *Macbeth* by name as they think it is bad luck, but simply call it 'The Scottish Play'. People associated with the play have died in mysterious circumstances, including the actor playing Lady Macbeth in the first ever performance of the play.

Others argue that there are so many accidents associated with *Macbeth* because it is a play set so much in the dark that actors can't properly see what they are doing backstage.

People in Shakespeare's time certainly believed in witches and Shakespeare included spells in *Macbeth* like the one above right.

No one knows exactly when *Macbeth* was written, but it was probably in 1606. It was written for James I of England who was also James VI of Scotland – hence 'The Scottish Play'.

Some people think Shakespeare may not have written all the plays.

7.2 The bell invites me ...

Macbeth is a tragedy – a play where there will be a sad ending. The sad ending in a tragedy is usually caused by a tragic flaw in the main character.

In Macbeth's case, he is ambitious to be king, and you might say that he loved his wife too much so that she was able to control his actions. Macbeth is a tragic hero.

CHALLENGE >>

Find out which other plays written by Shakespeare are tragedies.

Plays need performance

Shakespeare didn't write his plays for pupils to study in their English lessons! He wrote them to be performed and to entertain people.

Look at the extract on the right. Macbeth and Lady Macbeth are deciding to kill King Duncan. Have a go at acting it out with a partner.

CHALLENGE >>

In this extract Lady Macbeth says much more than her husband and she is obviously very excited. Write detailed notes for two actors playing the parts, explaining the background to this scene and giving instructions on how they should deliver their speeches. Which lines should Lady Macbeth particularly emphasise?

LADY MACBETH
Great Glamis! worthy Cawdor!
Greater than both, by the all-hail
hereafter!
Thy letters have transported me
beyond
This ignorant present, and I feel now
The future in the instant.

MACBETH
My dearest love,
Duncan comes here to-night.

LADY MACBETH
And when goes hence?

MACBETH
To-morrow, as he purposes.

LADY MACBETH
O, never
Shall sun that morrow see!
Your face, my thane, is as a book
where men
May read strange matters. To beguile
the time,
Look like the time; bear welcome in
your eye,
Your hand, your tongue: look like
the innocent flower,
But be the serpent under't. He that's
coming
Must be provided for: and you shall
put
This night's great business into my
dispatch;
Which shall to all our nights and
days to come
Give solely sovereign sway and
masterdom.

MACBETH
We will speak further.

LADY MACBETH
Only look up clear;
To alter favour ever is to fear:
Leave all the rest to me.

7.3 He can report ...

Have you ever been told off or praised for your spelling and handwriting?

Shakespeare's writing wasn't exactly tidy by modern standards! Look at the version of his signature on the right. It's not the best handwriting you've ever seen, is it?

Not only was Shakespeare an untidy writer, but he didn't always spell his name the same way. There is a lot of argument about which signatures are real and which are fake, but it seems that if there wasn't enough room to write his name in full Shakespeare simply changed the spelling to fit the space on the parchment! Many different versions have been found, including: William Shaksper, William Shakespeare, Willm Shakp, Wm Shakespe and William Shakespere.

▲ Shakespeare's signature

CHALLENGE >>

Shakespeare often made up new words when he was not satisfied with the power of existing words to capture his true meaning. With a partner discuss the advantages and disadvantages of this.

> Suggest some ground rules for making up new words.

> Make up five new words to express personal feelings and say why they should be adopted.

CHALLENGE >>

Think about spellings that, like Shakespeare, you might have difficulty with – especially words that sound the same but have different meanings.

For example:

Here = the place or location

(Try linking this with w<u>here</u> and <u>there</u>)

Hear = what we do with our ears

Remember that we h<u>ear</u> with our <u>ears</u>.

Make a list of your own personal spelling difficulties and try different ways to learn them. You might have a go at mnemonics, where the letters of the word spell out a sentence, like this:

Necessary – Never eat chocolate – eat simple salads and remain young.

Or you could try pictures, as it is double letters that often catch people out: Think of one collar and two sleeves in ne<u>cess</u>ary.

7.4 This dead butcher and his fiendlike queen

★ Hot-seating

★ Hot-seating is a technique used in drama where someone answers questions as if they were a character from the play.

There was a real Macbeth who was King in Scotland from 1040 to 1057. This Macbeth had killed King Duncan I in 1040. Duncan had also reigned for 17 years. In 1057, Macbeth was killed by Malcolm Canmore, who was Duncan's son. Shakespeare took some of these facts for his play.

CHALLENGE >>

Imagine you were writing a play about events in today's world. What would you choose to write about? Why?

> Make a list of three important characters you would need to put in it and briefly say what kind of people they are.
> Discuss the opening scene's importance in establishing the setting and introducing characters and themes.
> Plan out the opening scene that will make the biggest impact.

Write the opening scene of your play. Remember the rules of writing a play:

1 Begin with a person's name in bold before what they say.
2 Don't use speech marks.
3 Don't use 'said'.
4 Put stage directions in brackets.

When a character in a play says something that only the audience can hear, and not the other characters on stage, this is called an **aside**.

If a character is alone on stage, their speech is called a **soliloquy**. This is when they say what they really think and feel. The audience gets to know how they are feeling, but other characters in the play do not.

CHALLENGE >>

How do you think Banquo would answer these questions?

1 How did you feel when the witches said your children would be kings?
2 How did you think Macbeth reacted to the three prophecies given by the witches?
3 Who do you think murdered Duncan and why did they do it?

CHALLENGE > >

Look at Macbeth's soliloquy beginning 'Is this a dagger which I see before me'. What do you think he really thinks and feels at this point in the play?

7.5 Where the place?

When King Duncan has been murdered by Macbeth, all of nature is horrified because Macbeth has gone against God. Look again at what Lennox has to say about the night that Duncan was murdered:

The night has been unruly: where we lay,
Our chimneys were blown down; and, as they say,
Lamentings heard i' the air; strange screams of death,
And prophesying with accents terrible
Of dire combustion and confused events
New hatch'd to the woeful time: the obscure bird
Clamour'd the livelong night: some say, the earth
Was feverous and did shake.

CHALLENGE >>

Imagine you are Lennox. Write your diary for the day King Duncan has been murdered. Include the strange weather and peculiar happenings earlier in the day as well as the discovery of Duncan's body. Say how you feel about the killing of such a good man and what you think about the way Macbeth has behaved.

CHALLENGE >>

Imagine you were making a television or cinema version of the play.

> Discuss with a partner how you would film this speech if you were co-directors.
> Make a list of what you require to set the scene and create the right atmosphere.
> Give instructions for the composer about what kind of music you need to accompany each image.
> You can use the storyboard frame like the one below to sketch out how you think this speech would look as scenes in a film or television programme.

Storyboard

Scene one	Scene two	Scene three	Scene four
Scene five	Scene six	Scene seven	Scene eight

7.6 It will have blood they say, blood will have blood

Like Shakespeare, lots of modern authors use images (or word pictures) of blood and gore in their writing to gain the interest of their readers.

> The farmer was lying on the floor on the other side of the bed, partly covered by a sheet. He was obviously dead. Something – some sort of animal – had torn into his face and neck. There were hideous red gashes in his skin and his fair hair was matted with blood.
> His eyes were bulging, staring vacantly, and his mouth was forced open in a last attempt at a scream. His hands were stiff and twisted in a frantic effort to ward off something.

▲ Anthony Horowitz

CHALLENGE >>

Read the extract on the left from *Raven's Gate* by Anthony Horowitz and see if you can see where there are similarities with Shakespeare's language describing Banquo.

Shakespeare also used similar themes to those in Macbeth in his other plays. In the same way that he uses the ghost of Banquo as part of the theme of the supernatural in *Macbeth*, there is a ghost in *Hamlet*.

> Two nights together had these gentlemen,
> Marcellus and Bernardo, on their watch,
> In the dead vast and middle of the night,
> Been thus encounter'd. A figure like your father,
> Armed at point exactly, cap-a-pe,
> Appears before them, and with solemn march
> Goes slow and stately by them: thrice he walk'd
> By their oppress'd and fear-surprised eyes,
> Within his truncheon's length; whilst they, distilled
> Almost to jelly with the act of fear,
> Stand dumb and speak not to him. This to me
> In dreadful secrecy impart they did;
> And I with them the third night kept the watch;
> Where, as they had deliver'd, both in time,
> Form of the thing, each word made true and good,
> The apparition comes: I knew your father;
> These hands are not more like.

CHALLENGE >>

Hamlet has learnt that his father's ghost has been seen. Read the extract on the left out loud. It describes what has been seen.

CHALLENGE >>

Script the scene in the guardroom of the Castle at Elsinore that might have taken place when Marcellus and Bernardo, two soldiers who have been on watch, come off duty and attempt to tell fellow soldiers what they have just seen on the battlements.

7.7 The multitudinous seas incarnadine

As you know, Shakespeare invented all kinds of words, including insults.

We know the word 'fish' as a noun (thing) – a living creature and as a verb (action) – 'to fish'. Shakespeare invented the verb 'fishify', meaning to make something or someone fishy or fish-like.

Throughout your writing at secondary school, you will often be reminded to use 'the rule of 3' in your writing and speaking. The number 3 is thought to have special powers. The ancient Greeks used the three unities in their plays. These were time, place and action, which meant that all the action should be central to the plot, should take place in one location and happen in one day. In Christianity there is a holy trinity (3) of Father, Son and Holy Ghost. Writers and speakers have always continued to use 3s in their work.

CHALLENGE >>

1 See if you can get the word 'fishify' into a conversation.
2 Invent a new word and meaning and try to get it into the language so that other people use it too.

Think about how many times 3 has been used in stories you may know.
- How many little pigs were there?
- How many bears did Goldilocks meet?
- How many wishes do people usually get in fairy stories?
- How many lions are there on the England football shirt?
- How many musketeers were there?
- How many Wise Men?

Yes, you're right – the answer to all of these questions is – 3!

Did you know that Earth is the third planet from the sun?

Think about *Macbeth* and how Shakespeare uses the number 3:
- Macduff says, 'O horror! horror! horror!' when King Duncan is found murdered. Shakespeare uses repetition for effect and to emphasise his point.
- The play opens with three witches.
- The witches give Macbeth three prophecies.

▲ Three Lions

CHALLENGE >>

What were the three prophecies the witches gave to Macbeth immediately after the battle at the beginning of the play? Make a note of them and then write a soliloquy in which Macbeth anxiously goes over in his mind what the prophecies might mean and how things might turn out.

Extending

CHALLENGE >>

How many words can you make out of

WILLIAM SHAKESPEARE?

You may only use each letter the number of times it appears in the name and you may not have proper nouns.

Look up the word 'ambitious' in a dictionary.

One of the things we can say about Macbeth is that he is ambitious – he wants to become king. This is why he kills King Duncan and goes back to ask the three witches for more help.

- What ambitions do you have?
- Are they realistic?
- What do you intend to do to make them happen?
- What are the advantages of aiming high and having big ambitions?
- Can you think of any possible disadvantages?
- Why?

When Macbeth first meets the witches at the beginning of the play, he has just won the battle against the Thane of Cawdor. He writes to his wife, Lady Macbeth, and tells her what has happened. The witches have predicted his future.

Read the letter he sends:

CHALLENGE > >

1 Imagine Macbeth is going to write to Lady Macbeth after he has been back to the witches for a second time. Write the letter he would send to her, explaining the three new prophecies.

2 Towards the end of the play Macbeth discovers that the witches have deliberately misled him and encouraged him to have dishonourable ambitions. Make a list of all the evil deeds he commits in order to fulfil his ambitions.

They met me in the day of success: and I have learned by the perfectest report, they have more in them than mortal knowledge. When I burned in desire to question them further, they made themselves air, into which they vanished. Whiles I stood rapt in the wonder of it, came missives from the king, who all-hailed me 'Thane of Cawdor;' by which title, before, these weird sisters saluted me, and referred me to the coming on of time, with 'Hail, king that shalt be!' This have I thought good to deliver thee, my dearest partner of greatness, that thou mightst not lose the dues of rejoicing, by being ignorant of what greatness is promised thee. Lay it to thy heart, and farewell.

7.9 A tale told ...

Did you know that people in Shakespearean England thought there was a Chain of Being? This was an order of society like a long chain of links where everyone fitted. This meant that everyone had a place and they were not allowed to move out of it. It went something like this:

God ➔ Angels ➔ Kings ➔ Knights ➔ Squires or Lords of the manner ➔ Gentry or landowners ➔ Yeomen (free men with responsibilities) ➔ Tenants (without land of their own) ➔ Skilled labourers ➔ Unskilled labourers ➔ Women ➔ Animals ➔ Plants ➔ The Devil and demons in Hell

Kennings

Beowulf is written with lots of kennings. Kennings are invented descriptions made up of other existing words. The idea is that kennings help the listener or reader to picture the description better. An old English example is *banhus*, meaning 'bone house' – or 'human body'.

Kennings can just be two words linked together with a hyphen.

For example, a 'wind-dancer' could mean kite.
Or a rat might be a 'secret-sewer-dweller'.
Perhaps a 'game-ruiner' might be your little brother or sister.
You will probably have heard of a 'people-carrier' as a type of car.

Heroic Couplet

The Canterbury Tales are written in heroic couplets – pairs of lines that rhyme at the end and have 10 syllables in each line.

> A knight there was, and what a gentleman,
>
> Who, from the moment that he first ....

Alliteration

Sir Gawain and the Green Knight is an alliterative poem – lots of the words begin with the same consonant sound. (Think of She sells seashells on the seashore.)

CHALLENGE >>

Invent some kennings of your own to describe the following:
> the taste of your favourite drink
> a strong wind
> the sound of a police siren
> a pile of new coins
> two or three things or experiences of your own choice.

CHALLENGE >>

1 See if you can count the syllables and complete the heroic couplet on the left.
2 Write heroic couplets to describe a famous pop singer, a well-known politician, your favourite teacher, a person you most admire and, finally, yourself.

CHALLENGE >>

Write a few lines of poetry about a hero or heroine, using alliteration.

E x t e n d i n g

7.10 The time is free

CHALLENGE >>

The sonnet below has been set to music and turned into a song by lots of different artists.

1 Which group or singer would you choose to sing it in today's world? Give reasons for your choice.
2 Which band or singer is the best producer of love songs at the moment? Give reasons for your choice.
3 Take a modern song which you know well and have a go at rewriting it with some of the features you associate with Shakespeare.

You could have a go at writing some love song lyrics yourself. Or maybe you could try to write a sonnet in exactly the same format as Shakespeare used in his.

You never know, you could become as famous!

★ Love sonnets

★ Shakespeare didn't just write plays. He also wrote poems, particularly love sonnets. The sonnet below on the left is one of Shakespeare's most famous love sonnets.

CHALLENGE >>

1 Read the sonnet carefully and see if you can write down its main features. Shakespeare's sonnets were all written in the same way. See if you can work out how Shakespeare composed a sonnet. Think about iambic pentameter that you have already heard about, look carefully at how the sonnet rhymes and see how many rhymes there are.
2 Remember that sonnets do not necessarily have to be about love and can be about anything. Have a go at writing a sonnet on a different theme.

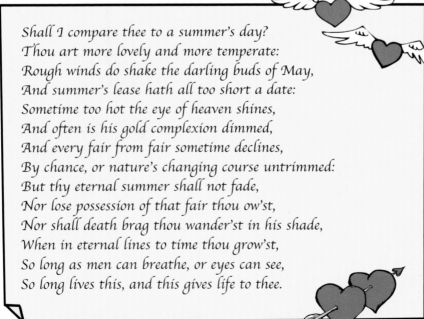

Shall I compare thee to a summer's day?
Thou art more lovely and more temperate:
Rough winds do shake the darling buds of May,
And summer's lease hath all too short a date:
Sometime too hot the eye of heaven shines,
And often is his gold complexion dimmed,
And every fair from fair sometime declines,
By chance, or nature's changing course untrimmed:
But thy eternal summer shall not fade,
Nor lose possession of that fair thou ow'st,
Nor shall death brag thou wander'st in his shade,
When in eternal lines to time thou grow'st,
So long as men can breathe, or eyes can see,
So long lives this, and this gives life to thee.

8.1 Exploring key concepts

The language of the web

Later in this unit you will be asked to create a website of your own. Impress the rest of your group with your knowledge of technical terms ...

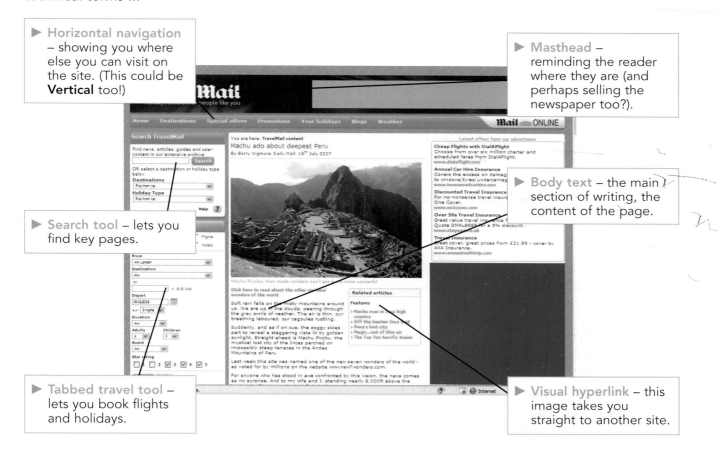

► **Horizontal navigation** – showing you where else you can visit on the site. (This could be **Vertical** too!)

► **Masthead** – reminding the reader where they are (and perhaps selling the newspaper too?).

► **Search tool** – lets you find key pages.

► **Body text** – the main section of writing, the content of the page.

► **Tabbed travel tool** – lets you book flights and holidays.

► **Visual hyperlink** – this image takes you straight to another site.

CHALLENGE >>

1 Go on the web and find examples of travel websites for yourself. See if you can use the terms above to label one or two pages.

2 Refer back to the work in the class lesson. What modes of communication are these elements using?

3 Now think about the effect of each of these elements. Which ones would you most like to use in your website, and why?

4 Try to mock up the home page of your website using as many of the features you have noted above as you think will work well. Either do this on your computer or as a diagram on a piece of paper.

Extending

8.2 Exploring printed travel texts

In the class lesson, you studied a travel blog about a couple who had visited Machu Picchu in Peru and looked at the man's viewpoint. Now it is time to analyse the woman's point of view.

This exercise will help you to see the link between what the writer says and what she is thinking. The first paragraph has been text-marked for you.

► The writer adds details to suggest that they are not fit enough for this journey. She is worried.

► She adds to this image by describing how quickly she got into trouble. She is referring to herself now rather than to her and Todd. Was she in a bit of a panic?

► She has made it and is feeling much better, if exhausted. Her mood is much more positive about the rest of the journey.

She said:

After just 36 hours in Cusco to acclimatize, we set off on our 4-day trek down the Inca Trail to Machu Picchu. In the almost 11 months of our trip, we have been extremely sporadic about exercising, and let's just say that we have both been in better physical shape than we are right now. After only two hours into the first day of hiking, I was already having trouble catching my breath in the altitude, while Todd was WAY ahead … By the time we got to the campsite the first night, my hiking boots and me were both absolutely wrecked! But luckily it wasn't anything that super glue, duct tape and a good night's sleep couldn't fix.

CHALLENGE >>

1 Use this example to add information to the following table:

Paragraph	Line from the text	Her thoughts	Her feelings
1	'After just 36 hours … to acclimatize …'	She is emphasising how they have not had enough time to get ready for this trek.	I think she is worried and nervous about whether they can do this.

2 Now complete the grid using ideas from the rest of this text.

By the second day, my altitude issues were over, and I was free to focus all my energy on the 5,000 or so feet that we had to climb. The last 2 hours of the uphill part of the hike were absolutely grueling … It was so steep in some parts that crawling on your hands and knees actually seemed like a good option … I nearly broke into tears when we got to camp that night.

On the third day, I started wondering if we were ever going to get there. It was the longest trek day (15km), and we hiked for almost 9 hours … The last two hours were really difficult (2000 or so steps downhill), and by the end we were alternating between insanely laughing and whimpering. I just kept reminding myself that we paid to do this, and that if I could get to the campsite, there was a hot shower waiting there.

3 Now use these ideas to write a paragraph explaining how the writer's mood changes during the extract.

4 Re-read the first extract, then research some background information on the Inca Trail: www.raingod.com/incatrail. Imagine you are starting out on it and write your first blog entry.

8.3 Exploring travel podcasts

Catching and keeping audience interest

In the class lesson, you listened to two extracts from the podcasts about Dublin. Below is a transcript of another section of the *Independent*'s Dublin podcast.

Temple Bar – the farmers' market

Time for a bite to eat! And if you are in Dublin on a Saturday, just aim for the middle of Temple Bar … On Saturday it comes alive with a farmers' market – I'm just seeing some wonderful looking organic mushrooms, beautiful aubergines, courgettes, wholemeal carrot cake. Oh, five euros for that looks like pretty good value, and then something a little more exotic; green olive paste!

But what if you fancy something a little more substantial in the terms of the best of dining options? That's why I've been summoned here to the opulent surroundings of the Merrion Hotel … I am in a beautiful drawing room; heavy curtains, very elegant fixtures and fittings …

CHALLENGE >>

1   Can you match the 'hooks' (listed below) with the right part of the transcript above?
> Vocabulary chosen to make the audience feel hungry
> Personal information to engage the audience
> Lists used to build up the image of the amount of items.
> Written in the first person to add to the listeners' relationship with the speaker.
> Short sentences to grab the listeners' attention
> Questions used to involve the listener in the action.
> Tense chosen to make it seem as if it is happening now.

2   Imagine you are producing the podcast for this section. What sound effects would you add and why?
Copy and complete this grid.

Sentence	Sound effect	Effect on the listener?

3   To accompany this podcast on the website, the designers want one image which can be used as a hotlink. What image should they use to best sum up what this extract is about and catch the interest of potential listeners?

4   Imagine there is a competition to provide the best hotlink. Write a paragraph to convince the judges yours is the best.

E x t e n d i n g

8.4 Creating travel podcasts

Travel podcast expert

In the class lesson, you have learnt to be an expert in creating exciting and informative podcasts.

Look at the details of the location below.

COCOLOCO'S WORLD OF CLOWNING

- fun-filled circus themed leisure park
- located close to major road and rail networks
- family tickets at a reduced rate
- three new rides this season
- two themed restaurants with children's meals and highchairs available
- hourly clowning shows in the Big Top
- clown face painting and dressing up sessions
- monorail to all major locations in the park
- clown schools for children in school holidays

Now look below at the existing travel podcast about CocoLoco's World of Clowning. This is downloadable from a website aimed at families who are looking for exciting day trips out.

> CocoLoco's World of Clowning has lots for people to do. The clowns are not as scary as some people think they are and hardly any children cry. There are rides and a Big Top to go into. There are places to eat and it is easy to get to. Go there; it is quite fun.

CHALLENGE >>

1. This is not very successful as a podcast. As an expert, write a report on it, outlining its weaknesses and suggesting improvements.
2. Now put these improvements into place, editing, changing and adding to the podcast to make it more suitable for its audience and purpose. You have a 200-word maximum.
3. Now consider the improvements and explain where and how yours is much better.

8.5 Exploring moving image travel texts – part 1

In the class lesson, you have been watching a film about the Neapolitan coast in Italy. The following tasks will help you to begin to write an interesting and detailed analysis of the film to answer the following question:

How does the moving image travel film you have studied make the audience feel about the Neapolitan coast?

CHALLENGE >>

1 Look at the images below. Make a note in your book of what camera shots and angles have been used.
2 Now add to your notes as many effects the images have on the intended audience as you can.
3 Consider another image from the film that you think had a powerful effect on the audience and repeat the process.
4 You now have four images to write about – and that is your essay ready to plan! Look back over your notes so far and decide on your overview of the film to complete this sentence:

> The moving image travel text about Neapolitan coast is aimed at a _____ audience and its purpose is to _____.

You now have the start of your essay. It is important that you remember this sentence because you will need to return back to it at the end of every paragraph.

5 Look over your notes. Decide on the best order to write them in order to explain your views clearly. List them in the order you will write about them in your books, and write a topic sentence for each. Each of these will be one paragraph in your finished piece.
6 Now begin drafting the first paragraph.

8.6 Exploring moving image travel texts – part 2

On the previous page you began to think about and plan your response to the essay question on the Neapolitan coast.

CHALLENGE >>

1 Now it is time to start putting your ideas into paragraphs. Look at the first point on the list you made in the last lesson and think carefully about it.

2 Below is an example of how a paragraph should look. Write your first idea in the same way in your books:

What do I have to do?		Example
Point	The idea you want to discuss in this paragraph	The film makes the audience feel very relaxed as they watch the film. *This can be seen when there is a shot at the beginning of the film of the water panning up to the town and this image is held for a long time.* The slow move of the camera and the long transition to the next shot slows the film down. Showing the calm water and the sleepy town shows the audience just how restful a holiday on the Neapolitan coast would be.
Evidence	*A description of the shot you are discussing*	
Explanation	Answering the question – how does what you have just written make the audience feel?	

Warning! Before you move on, go back to the question and check that you have answered it.

3 Now you are ready to write up your other ideas in the same way. Try to link each paragraph so that your writing flows. Some starters that might help you are:
> Another way the film influences the mood is …
> Later in the film …
> However, the mood changes when …

4 If you put this together with your introduction, you have nearly a completed essay. You just need a conclusion! Read through your essay so far. Then add a final paragraph summing up your view and considering which image or technique is most successful in influencing the audience's mood.

5 Now re-read the entire essay and check that all your points have been supported by **point**, **evidence** and **explanation**. Do this by underlining point, evidence, and explanation, using the colour code above.

8.7 Creating moving image travel texts

Changing images into text

In the class lesson, you will have thought very carefully about the meaning of images. As well as looking at what is shown in stills, you have also considered the impact of the angle, direction, and distance from the object to the camera.

In your discussions you have looked at all of these things. However, the time has come to turn the images into words that best describe the image. Look carefully at the image on the right.

CHALLENGE >>

1 Copy and complete this grid in your book.

	Description	Effect – how does it persuade the audience to visit the location?
Image colour – use of light and shade		
Camera shot – close-up, medium shot, long shot, etc.		
Camera angle – low, high, etc.		

2 In your opinion, which of these sentences best represents the image?

  a The green water lapped angrily at the windswept beach.

  b In the heat of the midday sun, the waves lapped lazily on the burning sand.

  c Far below in the bay, the white crests of the waves tickled at the golden sand.

3 Copy your chosen line into your book. Text-mark around it, showing how it represents the ideas you wrote in the grid.

4 Use all the ideas you considered above to create a fantastic piece of writing that will persuade the reader to want to visit the location.

CHALLENGE >>

You have been asked to work on a short film promoting your local shopping centre. Draw a chart: in column 1 list the five things you want to include in the film; in column 2 describe how you want each thing to be presented and filmed; in column 3 explain the effect this would have and how it would persuade people to visit.

Extending

8.8 Mapping the structure of a travel website

The structure of a website is very important. Put in too much information and people get confused; not enough, and they are bored, and will surf to another website before you can say 'Machu Picchu'!

The following website has been half planned. However, there are some big gaps and some ideas that the creators of the website were unable to decide what to do with.

CHALLENGE >>

1 Copy the following tree structure into your books. Fill it in, adding any other details you think would appeal to the target audience.

Notes

The website is for people interested in going on a cruise for the first time.

The purpose is to get them to book one!

HOME PAGE

- Places to cruise
  - Europe
  - Caribbean
- Facts about cruising
- Competition – win a cruise!

?

Where can they book a cruise from on this site? We need a link!

Other ideas

- blog from a first-time cruiser
- picture gallery
- podcast from a famous travel writer about a special cruise
- history of cruising
- promotional video from cruise companies

2 Having planned out what you intend to include in the website, write an invitation for people to contribute to it, listing the items you want and giving some explanation about what they should include, and their style and length.

8.9 Creating a travel website – part 1

Website research

In the class lesson, you have started to create a website of your own. The best way to improve your work is to examine as many sites as you can. Look at sites that are both similar to and different from yours for ideas.

CHALLENGE >>

1 Log on to a search engine. Look up websites that are either related to travel or to the subject area of your website.
2 Copy the table below. Use it to fill in your ideas as you surf the most interesting site.

Site name		Reason for choosing it	
Audience			
Purpose			
Multimodality			
Ideas for my site			

3 Consider the structure of the site and complete a tree structure to illustrate it. Here's an example to get you started:

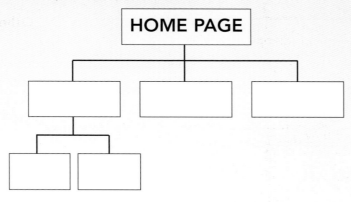

4 Now look for structures within the tree that would work well in your website and make a note of them, explaining exactly why and how they would work.
5 Repeat the whole process with a very different website and gather more ideas to share with your group next lesson.
6 Make a list of the five best ideas you have seen, saying how you can adopt them for your website.

Extending

8.10 Creating a travel website – part 2

Calling all travel multimodality experts!

Dear Expert

Below are the details of a new website planned for release very soon. We need a **travel multimodality expert** to analyse our plans and write a report. This should tell us what works on the website, and what still needs some attention. Please feel free to suggest changes!

Yours faithfully

The People of Dullsburgh

- **purpose:** to persuade people to visit our town – Dullsburgh
- **audience:** all ages
- **domain name:** www.dullsburgh.co.uk
- **tag line:** we don't have one!
- **tree structure:** see left

CHALLENGE > >

1 Now it is over to you. Write your report with the following headings:
  > successes
  > current weaknesses
  > suggestions for changes with explanations.

2 If you do not already have your own website, you are now in a position to actually create one. Discuss with a partner the kind of items you will need to put on it to reflect not only your own interests but to make it interesting for other people as well, including those who don't know you. Draw up a list of things you will need to include.

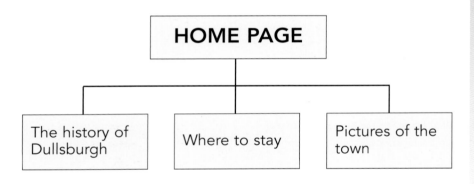

Home page

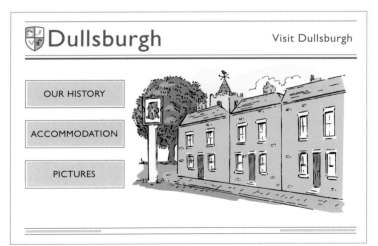

9.1 Asking the questions

Which is which?

Match the three descriptions below (a, b and c) to one of these three items:

1 British Isles   **2** Great Britain   **3** United Kingdom

a A group of islands comprising Great Britain, Ireland and a number of smaller islands. The group also includes the crown dependencies of the Isle of Man and the Channel Islands.

b The island of Great Britain, the northeast part of the island of Ireland and many small local islands.

c The combination of England, Scotland and Wales, including a number of outlying islands such as the Isle of Wight, Anglesey, the Isles of Scilly, the Hebrides, and the island groups of Orkney and Shetland, but not the Isle of Man or the Channel Islands.

★ Language

★ The original inhabitants of these islands were the Celts, but when Britain was invaded by the Romans they retreated, and their language forms the basis of Welsh and Gaelic. Over the centuries, Britain has been invaded many times. As each set of invaders brought their own language with them, the language we now know as English changed and absorbed new words.

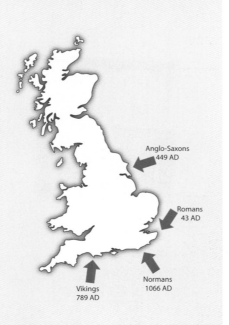

Anglo-Saxons
449 AD

Romans
43 AD

Normans
1066 AD

Vikings
789 AD

CHALLENGE > >

> New words are still entering the language all the time – these new words usually relate to things like food, sport, music and popular culture.
> Can you identify which language each of these three words comes from?
bistro (1922)
cappuccino (1948)
karaoke (1979)
> No one knows just how many different languages are spoken in Britain today. How many can you think of?
> One of the results of this process is that English has more **synonyms** than any other language. A synonym is a word that means the same as another – for example, 'big' and 'large'.
> How many synonyms can you think of for these words?
small   old   thin

CHALLENGE > >

In many parts of Wales, Welsh is spoken and Gaelic still survives in parts of Ireland, Scotland and the Isle of Man.

> Do some research to find out about where these languages are still spoken.
> On a map of the UK, colour code the places where the Celtic languages may be found.

Extending

9.2 Locating information

Did you know?

- The word 'alphabet' comes from the first two letters of the Greek alphabet – alpha (α) and beta (β).
- The longest alphabet in the world is the Cambodian one, which has 74 letters. The shortest is the Rotokas alphabet, which is the native language of the Solomon Islands, with just 11 letters.
- There are more than 2,700 languages in the world.
- All pilots on international flights identify themselves in English.
- English, the second most spoken language in the world, has more words than any other language. However, English speakers generally use only about one per cent of the language.
- The word 'Goodbye' came from 'God bye', which came from 'God be with you'. 'So long' came from the Arabic word 'salaam' and the Hebrew word 'shalom'.
- The longest non-medical word in the English language is 'floccinaucinihilipilification', which means 'the act of estimating as worthless'.
- The only 15-letter word that can be spelled without repeating a letter is 'uncopyrightable'.

Tips

Here are some tips to help you with your research. The most effective researchers:

- take time to plan
- find a question that is both challenging and possible, both open and focused
- explore many kinds of sources, not just textbooks
- find relevant information quickly
- think analytically and imaginatively about what they find
- store their notes in efficient and interesting ways
- collaborate with others and take on other people's views
- present their final ideas in inspiring and effective ways
- use what they find to solve a problem or make a difference.

CHALLENGE >>

Look up the following words in a dictionary or on the internet to find out where they come from or how they were made up:

- > vaccination
- > epidemic
- > anniversary
- > mutter
- > rendezvous
- > yacht
- > embark
- > fever

CHALLENGE >>

How well do you know your school library?

1 Write a brief guide to your school library or resource centre, include rules and opening times, as well as describing its key features. Draw a sketch map of it and mark on it the following:
  - > librarian's desk
  - > computers
  - > reference section
  - > non-fiction section
  - > fiction section
  - > reading area.
2 Discuss with your partner ways in which the library or resource centre could be improved and made more pupil-friendly.

9.3 Evaluating information

CHALLENGE >>

Scan the article below. Then answer these questions:

1 How many public libraries are there in the UK?
2 What sort of materials do libraries provide apart from books?
3 Which do people do more: go to the cinema, attend football matches, or visit libraries?
4 How useful is the information on the internet?
5 When was the internet invented?
6 How many homes in the UK had internet access in 2007?

The library versus the internet

Librarians say that most pupils start their research by using the internet, but basic information can often be quicker and easier to find in a book, such as an encyclopedia. Although the internet has become very popular, libraries are still a very valuable source of information.

- More than 60 per cent of the UK population hold a library ticket.
- 35 per cent of the UK population visit public libraries at least once a month.
- More people visit libraries than go to cinemas or attend football matches.
- In the UK, there are 92.4 million books in 3,500 public libraries and every year more than 318 million book loans.
- There are a further 34 million issues of other material, including DVDs, videos and talking books.
- UK library staff answer 58.5 million enquiries a year.
- Nearly 25,000 People's Network PC terminals are available in UK libraries for public use. Of these, 83 per cent are free of charge.

The internet has only existed for three decades, and the World Wide Web is younger still. In 2007, nearly 15 million households in the UK (61 per cent) had internet access. This is an increase of nearly 4 million households (36 per cent) since 2002. In 2007, 84 per cent of UK households with internet access had a broadband connection.

The internet has increased access to information around the world. However, the quality of the information on the web can vary enormously – from completely useless, or even damaging, to extremely valuable.

Today's search engines draw the most relevant information to our attention. The importance of search engines will increase as more data become available online. In the future, people around the world will need to look for new ways to identify the accuracy of online information sources.

CHALLENGE >>

Sometimes it becomes temporarily impossible to access the internet. Discuss with a partner how you would cope with this, if you were in the school library or resource centre doing an urgent project for your favourite subject.

9.4 Making notes

Shorthand

Shorthand is a form of writing that uses symbols or abbreviations for words and common phrases. It allows someone who is well trained in the system to write as quickly as most people speak.

The term 'shorthand' is often used now to refer to the abbreviated messages typed back and forth via Instant Messaging.

One of the most common abbreviations used by internet users is the 'at' symbol (@). Computer engineer Ray Tomlinson is credited with inventing its use in this way in 1971, when he grappled with how to properly address what would be history's very first email.

CHALLENGE >>

1 Do you know the meaning of these common abbreviations?
   > RIP   > RSVP
   > BBC   > FBI
   > VIP   > MP
   > am   > anon
2 Make up three or four useful abbreviations to represent common sayings or things. Make them easy to remember.

Textspeak

Textspeak is a form of shorthand with which most young people are familiar. It is a way of shortening words and inserting numbers, usually into a text message.

> **gr8 u r cmin out 2nite. c u l8r. x**

CHALLENGE >>

1 Some older people might not understand textspeak. Produce an easy-to-follow guide to help them.
2 Write a text message to someone in your house saying what you would like to eat tonight. Imagine that if they cannot understand it, you will go hungry!

9.5 Assembling information

Planning tools

Look again at the planning tools you have been using in your class lesson:

Concept map

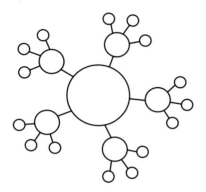

Tree diagram

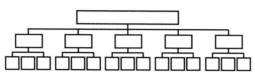

Tree map

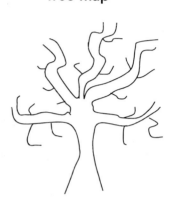

CHALLENGE >>

> Read the three topic cards below and categorise and link the words into a planning tool of your choice.
> You may need to add categories to build your plan. You might like to add things to the plan too.
> Remember that you can use images and symbols as well as words.
> Create your own topic card and then transfer it into a planning tool you have not worked with yet.

Books
Fiction
Novel
Humour
Oliver Twist
Encyclopedia
Dictionary
Non-fiction
Bible
Author
Publisher
Printer
His Dark Materials
Atlas
Horror

Hobbies
Equipment
Karate
Model-making
Outside activity
Kayaking
Team activity
Knitting
Clothing
Inside activity
Train-spotting
Video games
Basketball
Solo activity
Football

Holidays
Europe
Safety
Train
Transport
America
First aid kit
Package
Africa
Spain
Camping
Independent
Car
Vaccinations
Aeroplane

9.6 Learning about other cultures

Migration

People migrate for many reasons: to escape from a bad situation, to be with relatives, because of their job or for a better life, perhaps. It can be very difficult settling into a new country, and a new way of life. What do you think the main problems might be for people who move to another country?

This is how one teenager felt when she arrived in the UK.

DIARY   **DECEMBER 14ᵀᴴ**

I arrived in England in 1987 at the age of 15. Leaving Pakistan was a heartbreaking experience, as I was leaving my friends, family, school and the house I grew up in. Heathrow Airport greeted me with cold and misty weather, quite opposite of the hot climate in Pakistan. It was a big climate shock, and I wrapped myself in a shawl, but was still feeling very cold. My uncle came to the airport to receive me, and we started another never-ending road journey to Oldham. I felt hungry after a while and ate crisps and drank Coke from a tin for the very first time. It tasted very nice, but I became worried that in England this would be the normal food and perhaps I would not get my beloved curry and chappatis. During this journey I noticed everything was clean, tidy and new. All the roads had tarmac and I saw the motorway for the first time and the hills were green. It was a big culture shock to see women wearing mini-skirts, especially in the cold weather.

When I stepped inside the house, it felt strange walking on the carpet, as I was used to walking on tiled floors. I noticed all the houses and streets were the same, and I was afraid of getting lost if I went out. The house and the garden were very small, compared to the big house with a very large garden I had left behind.

CHALLENGE >>

> Make a list of what you would miss about your own country if you moved abroad, and put the items in order of importance.
> Imagine you have moved to another country. Write a letter to a friend, describing your feelings about your arrival in your new home and describing the things you are most missing.

★ The American Dream

★ In the first half of the 20th century, many people who faced terrible poverty in Europe decided to leave their homes and travel to America in pursuit of the 'American Dream'. The Statue of Liberty was the first thing they saw as the steamships that brought them to America entered New York Harbour.

Inside the base is a poem which includes these welcoming lines:

Give me your tired, your poor,
Your huddled masses yearning to breathe free,
The wretched refuse of your teeming shore.
Send these, the homeless, tempest-tost to me.

CHALLENGE >>

Write a humorous four-line verse, intended for new Year 7 pupils, about your school, its aims and policies.

9.7 Planning your documentary

Becoming a British citizen

Since 1 January 2004, all adults wishing to become British citizens in the UK have been required to attend a citizenship ceremony as the final stage in the process. As part of the ceremony they have to say either the oath or the affirmation, and the pledge.

Oath of allegiance

I [name] swear by Almighty God that I will be faithful and bear true allegiance to Her Majesty Queen Elizabeth, her Heirs and Successors, according to law. So help me God.

Affirmation of allegiance

I [name] do solemnly, sincerely and truly declare and affirm that on becoming a British citizen, I will be faithful and bear true allegiance to Her Majesty Queen Elizabeth the Second, her Heirs and Successors, according to law.

Pledge

I will give my loyalty to the United Kingdom and respect its rights and freedoms. I will uphold its democratic values. I will observe its laws faithfully and fulfil my duties and obligations as a British citizen.

During the ceremony speeches are made, often by local or national dignitaries. These may include welcoming the new citizens on behalf of the local area and encouraging them to play an active role within their communities.

The new citizens are presented with their certificate of British citizenship, and a welcome pack. A commemorative gift, often with a local flavour, may also be given. All new citizens are invited to stand while the National Anthem is played.

CHALLENGE >>

Imagine you were chosen to welcome to your school a new pupil who had just recently come to this country. Draft out the speech you would make, including details of your school's role within the community.

CHALLENGE >>

1 Find out the meanings of these words:
   > allegiance
   > Heirs and Successors
   > dignitaries
   > commemorative
2 People under 18 do not have to take part in a citizenship ceremony. But if they did, how might you change the oath, affirmation and pledge to make them easier to understand and more relevant for young people.
3 Write a speech of welcome for new citizens in your area.
4 Design the 'Welcome Pack' to give to new citizens. What would be an appropriate gift to include?
5 What do you think are the five most important qualities of being a good citizen? Discuss with your partner and write them down in order of importance.

9.8 Getting it right

In many cultures young people mark growing up by means of a 'coming of age' ceremony. Read these examples from around the world.

An Inuit boy, when he reaches the age of 11 or 12, is taken out into the wilderness by some of the men in his family to test his hunting skills. They will live in tents, play traditional games and eat what they catch, the elders passing on their knowledge to the young. Traditionally, the coastal Inuit men will take their sons on such a hunt as soon as they appear strong enough to undertake an arduous journey.

In the Dominican Republic, turning 15 is a huge step in a young girl's life. A family may celebrate by holding a *quinceañera* or *quince*, a celebration to mark their daughter's coming of age (*quince* means 'fifteen' in Spanish). This includes a Catholic Mass in honour of the girl, who then receives instruction of her new obligations as a woman. After her *quince*, the girl is able to attend social functions with her parents, have boyfriends, wear make-up and must accept the responsibilities of an adult.

A young Muslim girl in Malaysia will start to study the Koran at about four years of age and, when she has completed her study at about 11, she is honoured at the village mosque in an important ritual known as the Khatam Al Koran. She must recite verses from the final chapter of the Koran to all the people present. Afterwards, her family will celebrate with a meal.

In Jewish families the Bar Mitzvah is celebrated when a boy reaches the age of 13. In the ceremony, boys are called forward to read in Hebrew from the Torah scroll, the first five books of scripture known as the Books of Moses or the Law. This is a public announcement that they have come of age. The boy will then receive his father's blessing. The father thanks God that he has now been freed from responsibility for the boy's sins and rejoices that his son is now a man. After the ceremony the parents arrange a meal, called the Seudah, for all the boy's family and friends. The boy will deliver a sermon of thanks and receive gifts from his guests during this meal.

★ Coming of age

★ These features are common to many 'coming of age' rituals:
Contact with nature – for example, hunting or being left alone in the natural environment.
An ordeal or challenge – for example, a fast, all-night vigil or task. The challenge needs to be big enough so that it is new and significant, but not so great that failure is more likely than success.
Public witnesses – for example, an announcement, ceremony or gathering with family and friends.

CHALLENGE >>

1 Discuss with a partner the ceremonies on this page.
> What do you think they are intended to achieve?
> Do they have anything in common?
> Do you know of any other coming of age ceremonies?
2 Work with a partner to design a 'coming of age' ceremony for young Britons.

9.9 Presenting information

You are going on a Year 7 exchange visit to another country. As part of your brief you are asked to give an informative presentation using PowerPoint ® to promote your own country.

CHALLENGE >>

Plan what you will have on your slides and what you will say in the lines provided.

CHALLENGE >>

> Draw a spider diagram of the things you intend to include in your presentation.
> Plan out your talk, selecting and listing the points you will use to promote your country and noting down the essential information you will need to include.

Plan what you will include on each slide. It might help to sketch it first.

Write your notes for your presentation on a frame like this.

Read the information below about the opening ceremony of the Sydney Olympic Games in 2000.

Sydney 2000

The opening of the 27th Olympiad took place on Friday 15 December 2000 in the magnificent Olympic stadium of Sydney, built especially for this historic event. The stadium is 14.5 kilometres (9 miles) from the centre of the city and 1 million people were on the streets of Sydney the night before.

The ceremony, which lasted nearly four hours, started with horsemen entering the stadium bearing the Olympic flags, symbolising the arrival of horsemen in Australia in 1778. Following the Australian National Anthem, the story of Australia was portrayed through scenes of sea and fish, forest fires and dances by the Aborigines, the indigenous population of Australia for 40,000 years. The Olympic Anthem was sung in Greek by the Australian Greek Orthodox Church Choir.

The climax of the ceremony was the Olympic torch entering the stadium, relayed by veteran Australian Olympic athletes of the 20th century and handed over to the Australian athlete Cathy Freeman, the 400m world champion, who was ringed by fire after lighting the Olympic flame. The flames rose above her and moved up the stand to a final resting place over the stadium.

★ The Sydney Olympic Games

★ Built at a cost of more than £250 million, the new stadium has a capacity of 110,000. Four Boeing 747 aeroplanes would fit side by side under the span of the main arches of the grandstands.

★ Inside the stadium there are 99 tonnes of lighting and power equipment. These are connected by 3 kilometres (2 miles) of wiring.

★ A production crew of 4,600 people planned the ceremony.

★ The Olympic flame went on a 20,940-kilometre (16,740-mile) route across Australia involving 11,000 torchbearers and passing near 80 per cent of the population.

CHALLENGE >>

1 Imagine you have been asked to plan and write the proposal for the opening ceremony for the British Olympic Games in 2012. Remember: it must reflect Britain's multicultural character.

2 Look up the 'Olympic Charter' and with a partner discuss the Olympic universal values. You may need to look up some of the words in a dictionary.